# Blue Ribbon
## family favorites

Joan's Chicken
Stuffing Casserole,
page 217

# Blue Ribbon

## family favorites

Oxmoor
HOUSE®

# Blue Ribbon
## family favorites

©2012 by Gooseberry Patch
2500 Farmers Dr., #110, Columbus, Ohio 43235
1-800-854-6673, **gooseberrypatch.com**
©2012 by Time Home Entertainment Inc.
135 West 50th Street, New York, NY 10020

ISBN-13: 978-0-8487-3729-0
ISBN-10: 0-8487-3729-6
Library of Congress Control Number: 2011945598
Printed in the United States of America
First Printing 2012

**Oxmoor House**
VP, Publishing Director: Jim Childs
Creative Director: Felicity Keane
Brand Manager: Vanessa Tiongson
Senior Editor: Rebecca Brennan
Managing Editor: Rebecca Benton

**Gooseberry Patch Blue Ribbon Family Favorites**
Project Editor: Sarah H. Doss
Assistant Designer: Allison Sperando Potter
Director, Test Kitchen: Elizabeth Tyler Austin
Assistant Directors, Test Kitchen: Julie Christopher,
  Julie Gunter
Test Kitchen Professionals: Wendy Ball, R.D.;
  Allison E. Cox; Victoria E. Cox; Margaret Monroe
  Dickey; Alyson Moreland Haynes; Stefanie Maloney;
  Callie Nash; Catherine Crowell Steele;
  Leah Van Deren
Photography Director: Jim Bathie
Senior Photo Stylist: Kay E. Clarke
Associate Photo Stylist: Katherine Eckert Coyne
Assistant Photo Stylist: Mary Louise Menendez
Production Manager: Theresa Beste-Farley

**Contributors**
Editor: Natalie Kelly Brown
Photography: Brave Ink Press
Copy Editor: Jasmine Hodges
Proofreaders: Donna Baldone, Rhonda Lee Lother
Indexer: Mary Ann Laurens
Interns: Erin Bishop, Maribeth Browning, Mackenzie Cogle,
  Laura Hoxworth, Alicia Lavender, Alison Loughman,
  Anna Pollock, Ashley White
Test Kitchen Professionals: Martha Condra, Erica Hopper,
  Kathleen Royal Phillips
Photo Stylist: Mindi Shapiro-Levine

**Time Home Entertainment Inc.**
Publisher: Richard Fraiman
VP, Strategy & Business Development: Steven Sandonato
Executive Director, Marketing Services: Carol Pittard
Executive Director, Retail & Special Sales: Tom Mifsud
Director, Bookazine Development & Marketing:
  Laura Adam
Publishing Director: Joy Butts
Finance Director: Glenn Buonocore
Associate General Counsel: Helen Wan

To order additional publications, call 1-800-765-6400.
For more books to enrich your life, visit **oxmoorhouse.com**
To search, savor, and share thousands of recipes, visit **myrecipes.com**

Cover: People-Pleasin' Peach Pie (page 283)
Page 1: Blueberry-Citrus Cake (page 264)

# Dear Friend,

When it comes to good food, nothing satisfies quite like a home-cooked meal. Scattered throughout these pages is a treasured collection of tried & true recipes. Most start with common ingredients you'll already have on hand. And of course, we just had to include those clever decorating ideas as well as family memories from our recipe contributors.

Buttermilk Baked Chicken (page 146) is simplicity at its best. Need an irresistible side to go with a main dish? Serve Sweet & Nutty Couscous (page 180) or Zesty Horseradish Carrots (page 184). A bowl of Slow-Cooker Steak Chili (page 211) with a freshly baked corn muffin is one dish that delivers on comfort. Our *Easy Make-Ahead Meals & More* chapter is full of baked goods, home canning and gift-giving ideas to share with friends and family.

In need of a sweet ending? Our dessert chapter is full of delectable treats that can't be beat. Delight your taste buds with Caramel-Glazed Apple Cake (page 271), a yummy and moist cake topped with a warm and buttery glaze. Smooth and creamy Homemade Vanilla Ice Cream (page 306) will have the family ready and waiting with spoons and bowls as soon as the ice cream maker stops.

So take a peek inside…you'll find recipes that are simple to prepare yet deliver on taste and presentation. There are also cooking tips and techniques to help you put together great dishes with minimal fuss. From breakfast to sandwiches, old-time classics, delicious desserts and everything else in between, we're confident *Blue Ribbon Family Favorites* will be a go-to source on your kitchen bookshelf.

# From our families to yours,

### Vickie & JoAnn

# contents

Nutty Banana Shake, page 41

Pepper Steak Sammies, page 103

Penne with Sausage & Cheese, page 129

Easy Cherry Cobbler, page 290

Herbed Sausage Quiche

# all about
# breakfast &
# brunch

*Start your day off right with these tasty recipes. Breakfast Burritos (page 11) are easy to fix when you're in a hurry. You can freeze a batch ahead of time and then microwave them in two minutes. Having company over? Not a problem…you'll have plenty of delicious recipes to choose from that will satisfy any appetite. Packed with flavor, Yummy Brunch Strata (page 15) will have guests coming back for more. And for a great weekend treat, Creamy Cinnamon Rolls (page 32) just can't be beat.*

# Country-Style Breakfast Pizza

*A sure-fire breakfast hit...you'll get requests for this recipe!*

13.8-oz. tube refrigerated pizza
    crust dough
Optional: garlic salt
24-oz. pkg. refrigerated mashed
    potatoes
10 eggs, beaten

Optional: chopped vegetables,
    cooked ham or sausage
8-oz. pkg. shredded Colby Jack
    cheese
4-oz. pkg. crumbled bacon
    pieces

Spread pizza dough in a pizza pan sprayed with non-stick vegetable spray; sprinkle with garlic salt, if desired, and set aside. Place mashed potatoes in a microwave-safe bowl; microwave on high setting for about 5 minutes, or until heated through. Spread potatoes over dough. Cook eggs as desired, adding vegetables, ham or sausage, if desired. Spread scrambled eggs mixture evenly over potatoes. Sprinkle with cheese; top with bacon. Bake at 350 degrees for 12 to 15 minutes, until cheese is melted and crust is golden. Serves 8.

*Jackie Balla*
*Walbridge, OH*

## wake up with a smile

Surprise sleepyheads at breakfast...serve each a made-to-order omelet in a mini cast-iron skillet. A cheery red bandanna tied around the handle makes a nice napkin.

# Breakfast Burritos

16-oz. pkg. ground pork
    breakfast sausage
8-oz. pkg. shredded Mexican-
    blend cheese

10-oz. can diced tomatoes with
    green chiles, drained
5 eggs, beaten
8 10-inch flour tortillas

Brown sausage in a skillet over medium heat; drain. Combine sausage, cheese and tomatoes in a bowl. Cook eggs in same skillet. Add eggs to sausage mixture and mix thoroughly. Divide mixture evenly among tortillas and roll tightly. Seal tortillas by cooking for one to 2 minutes on a hot griddle sprayed with non-stick vegetable spray. Serves 8.

*Cherie White*
*Oklahoma City, OK*

# Herbed Sausage Quiche
(pictured on page 8)

*For a savory pie crust, spread 2½ tablespoons softened butter in a pie plate and firmly press 2½ cups buttery cracker crumbs or seasoned dry bread crumbs into the butter. Freeze until firm; pour in filling and bake as directed.*

9-inch frozen pie crust, thawed
1 c. ground pork breakfast
    sausage, browned and
    drained
3 eggs, beaten
1 c. whipping cream

1 c. shredded Cheddar cheese
1 sprig fresh rosemary, chopped
1½ t. Italian seasoning
¼ t. salt
¼ t. pepper

Bake pie crust according to package directions. In a bowl, mix together all ingredients except pie crust; spread into crust. Bake, uncovered, at 450 degrees for 15 minutes. Reduce heat to 350 degrees, cover with foil and bake for 9 more minutes. Cut into wedges to serve. Serves 8.

*Cherylann Smith*
*Efland, NC*

# Crab, Corn & Pepper Frittata

*When it is in season, use fresh corn.*

6 eggs, beaten
¼ c. milk
⅓ c. mayonnaise
2 T. green onions, chopped
2 T. red pepper, chopped
⅓ c. corn

salt and pepper to taste
1 c. crabmeat
1 c. shredded Monterey Jack
   cheese
Optional: chopped green onions

   Whisk together first 7 ingredients. Gently stir in crabmeat. Pour into a greased 10" pie plate. Bake at 350 degrees for 15 to 20 minutes. Sprinkle with cheese and bake for 5 more minutes, or until cheese is melted. Garnish with green onions, if desired. Serves 4 to 6.

*Stacie Avner*
*Delaware, OH*

## *outdoor garden on the move*

Recycle an old wheelbarrow into a movable garden filled with pots of herbs, flowers, lettuce or carrots... how clever!

# Summer Swiss Quiche

*This is an excellent breakfast or brunch dish to serve when the garden harvest kicks in.*

½ lb. bacon
2 zucchini, thinly sliced
1 green pepper, chopped
1 onion, chopped
1 to 2 T. butter or olive oil

8 eggs, beaten
1 c. milk
¼ c. biscuit baking mix
5 slices Swiss cheese

Cook bacon until crisp in a skillet over medium heat; drain and set aside. Sauté zucchini, green pepper and onion in butter or oil in a separate skillet over medium heat. Mix eggs, milk and baking mix in a bowl. Pour egg mixture into a lightly greased 13"x9" baking pan. Spoon zucchini mixture over egg mixture. Cover with crumbled bacon; arrange cheese slices on top. Bake, uncovered, at 350 degrees for 30 to 35 minutes, until a toothpick inserted near the center comes out clean. Cut into squares. Serves 8 to 10.

*Rebecca Barna*
*Blairsville, PA*

## just for you

Bake a quiche in muffin or custard cups for oh-so-simple individual servings. When making minis, reduce the baking time by about 10 minutes and check for doneness with a toothpick.

# Yummy Brunch Strata

*All you need to accompany this feed-a-crowd dish is a tray of sweet rolls, a big pot of hot coffee and fellowship!*

⅓ c. oil
2 c. cooked ham, diced
3 c. sliced mushrooms
3 c. zucchini, diced
1½ c. onion, diced
1½ c. green, red or yellow
　　pepper, diced
2 cloves garlic, minced

2 8-oz. pkgs. cream cheese,
　　softened
½ c. half-and-half
1 doz. eggs, beaten
4 c. day-old bread, cubed
3 c. shredded Cheddar cheese
salt and pepper to taste

Heat oil in a large skillet over medium-high heat. Add ham, vegetables and garlic. Sauté for 3 to 5 minutes, until tender. Drain; set aside. In a large bowl, beat together cream cheese and half-and-half with an electric mixer at medium speed. Stir in vegetable mixture and remaining ingredients; blend lightly. Pour into 2 greased 11"x7" baking pans. Bake, uncovered, at 350 degrees for 35 to 40 minutes, until a knife inserted near the center comes out clean. Let stand 10 minutes; cut into squares. Serves 16.

*Lynn Williams*
*Muncie, IN*

# California Omelet

1 T. oil
3 to 4 eggs
¼ c. milk
salt and pepper to taste

1 avocado, sliced
2 to 3 green onions, diced
½ c. shredded Monterey Jack
　cheese

Heat oil in a skillet over medium-low heat. Whisk together eggs, milk, salt and pepper in a bowl; pour into skillet. Cook until eggs are lightly golden on bottom and partially set on top. Sprinkle with remaining ingredients; carefully fold omelet in half so toppings are covered. Reduce heat to medium-low and cook, uncovered, about 10 minutes. Serves 2.

*Christina Mendoza*
*Alamogordo, NM*

We love breakfast foods, but it seems as if there's never enough time to linger over them in the morning. Enjoy an unhurried breakfast with your family...at dinnertime! An omelet or frittata is perfect. Just add a basket of muffins, fresh fruit and a steamy pot of tea.

# Mocha Muffins

2 c. all-purpose flour
¾ c. plus 1 T. sugar
2½ t. baking powder
1 t. cinnamon
½ t. salt
1 c. milk
2 T. plus ½ t. instant coffee
    granules, divided

½ c. butter, melted
1 egg, beaten
1½ t. vanilla extract, divided
1 c. mini semi-sweet chocolate
    chips, divided
½ c. cream cheese, softened

Whisk together flour, sugar, baking powder, cinnamon and salt in a large bowl. In a separate bowl, stir together milk and 2 tablespoons coffee granules until coffee is dissolved. Add butter, egg and one teaspoon vanilla; mix well. Stir into dry ingredients until just moistened. Fold in ¾ cup chocolate chips. Fill greased or paper-lined muffin cups ⅔ full. Bake at 375 degrees for 17 to 20 minutes for regular muffins or 13 to 15 minutes for mini muffins. Cool for 5 minutes before removing from pans to wire racks. Combine cream cheese and remaining coffee granules, vanilla and chocolate chips in a food processor or blender. Cover and process until well blended. Refrigerate spread until serving time. Serve spread on the side. Makes 16 regular or 36 mini muffins.

*Paige Woodard*
*Loveland, CO*

# Grandma Retha's Rhubarb Muffins

1 c. brown sugar, packed
1 egg, beaten
1 c. buttermilk
½ c. oil
2 t. vanilla extract
1½ c. rhubarb, diced
Optional: ½ c. chopped walnuts

2½ c. all-purpose flour
1 t. baking powder
1 t. baking soda
½ t. salt
1 t. butter, melted
½ c. sugar
1 t. cinnamon

Combine brown sugar, egg, milk, oil and vanilla in a large bowl; mix well. Stir in rhubarb and nuts, if desired. Combine flour, baking powder, baking soda and salt in a separate bowl; stir dry ingredients into rhubarb mixture. Spoon into greased muffin cups, filling ⅔ full. Stir together melted butter, sugar and cinnamon; sprinkle over muffins. Bake at 350 degrees for 20 to 25 minutes. Makes 12 to 15 large muffins.

*Emily Lynch*
*Iroquois, SD*

## get creative

Muffins just seem sweeter served from a create-your-own farmhouse-style muffin stand. Use household cement, found at hardware stores, to secure the bottom of a jadite teacup to the center bottom of a vintage plate. Let cement dry according to the manufacturer's instructions. When completely dry, arrange muffins on the plate and then top with a glass cake stand lid.

# Mile-High Buttermilk Biscuits

*The secret? Use a sharp biscuit cutter, and don't twist it when cutting out your biscuits...you'll be amazed how high they rise!*

2 c. all-purpose flour
1 T. baking powder
1 t. salt
½ c. shortening, chilled
    in freezer

⅔ to ¾ c. buttermilk
¼ c. butter, melted

Mix together flour, baking powder and salt. Cut in shortening until mixture has a crumbly texture. Stir in buttermilk until incorporated and dough leaves sides of bowl. Dough will be sticky. Knead dough 3 to 4 times on a lightly floured surface. Roll out to ½-inch thickness, about 2 to 4 passes with a rolling pin. Cut dough with a biscuit cutter, pressing straight down with cutter. Place biscuits on a parchment paper-lined baking sheet. Bake at 500 degrees for 8 to 10 minutes. Brush tops of warm biscuits with melted butter. Makes about one dozen.

*Staci Meyers*
*Montezuma, GA*

## make 'em tender

For the flakiest biscuits, stir just to moisten and gently roll or pat the dough...don't overmix it.

# Kathy's Bacon Popovers

*Mmm...bacon! An easy tote-along breakfast to enjoy on the go.*

2 eggs
1 c. milk
1 T. oil
1 c. all-purpose flour

½ t. salt
3 slices bacon, crisply cooked
   and crumbled

Whisk together eggs, milk and oil. Beat in flour and salt just until smooth. Fill 12 greased and floured muffin cups ⅔ full. Sprinkle bacon evenly over batter. Bake at 400 degrees for 25 to 30 minutes, until puffed and golden. Serve warm. Makes one dozen.

*Kathy Grashoff*
*Fort Wayne, IN*

# Chocolate-Cherry Cream Scones

*This recipe was passed on to me by a dear friend. These scones are absolutely irresistible, especially warm from the oven!*

*—Michelle*

2 c. all-purpose flour
1 T. baking powder
½ t. salt
¼ c. sugar
¼ c. mini semi-sweet chocolate
   chips

½ c. dried cherries, chopped
1¼ c. whipping cream
Garnish: additional whipping
   cream, coarse sugar

Combine flour, baking powder, salt and sugar in a bowl; whisk to blend well. Add chocolate chips and cherries. Pour cream into dry ingredients, continuing to stir until a soft, sticky dough is formed. Turn out onto a lightly floured surface and knead 8 to 10 times. Pat dough into a circle ½-inch to ¾-inch thick; cut into 8 wedges. Place wedges one inch apart on a parchment paper-lined baking sheet. Brush with additional cream; sprinkle generously with coarse sugar. Bake at 425 degrees for about 15 minutes, or until golden and springy to the touch. Makes 8.

*Michelle Stewart*
*West Richland, WA*

Kathy's Bacon Popovers

# Breakfast Berry Parfait

*So pretty served in parfait glasses or champagne flutes!*

1 c. strawberries, hulled
½ c. raspberries
¼ c. blackberries

1 c. bran & raisin cereal
6-oz. container strawberry
    yogurt

    Combine berries in a bowl. Top with cereal. Spoon yogurt over berry mixture. Serves 2.

*Michelle Case*
*Yardley, PA*

## hang it up

For fuss-free mornings, hang up a country-style peg rack by the back door...you'll always know where to find the kids' backpacks, umbrellas and even the dog's leash!

# Sweet & Spicy Bacon

*Try this easy-to-fix bacon at your next brunch...guests will love it!*

½ c. brown sugar, packed
2 T. chili powder
1 t. ground cumin
1 t. cumin seed

1 t. ground coriander
¼ t. cayenne pepper
10 thick slices bacon

Line a 15"x10" jelly-roll pan with aluminum foil. Place a wire rack on pan and set aside. Combine all ingredients except bacon. Sprinkle mixture onto a large piece of wax paper. Press bacon slices into mixture, turning to coat well. Arrange in a single layer on wire rack in pan; place pan on center rack of oven. Bake at 400 degrees for 12 minutes; turn bacon over. Bake for 10 more minutes, or until deep brown but not burned. Drain on paper towels; serve warm. Serves 4 to 5.

*Zoe Bennett*
*Columbia, SC*

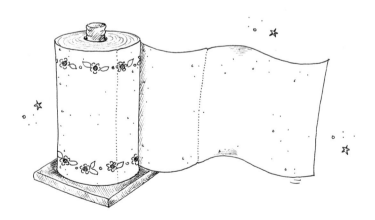

# Creamy Cheddar Grits

6 c. milk
6 c. water
2 t. salt
1 t. pepper
¼ c. butter, divided

1½ c. long-cooking grits, uncooked
16-oz. pkg. finely shredded Cheddar cheese

Combine milk, water, salt, pepper and 2 tablespoons butter in a large saucepan over medium heat. Bring to a low boil; whisk in grits. Reduce heat; simmer for one hour and 15 minutes, whisking occasionally. Remove from heat; stir in cheese and remaining butter. Serves 8.

*Dana Cunningham*
*Lafayette, LA*


# Oven-Fried Bacon Potatoes

6 to 8 potatoes, peeled and halved

3 T. butter, melted
4 to 6 slices bacon

Cook potatoes in boiling salted water until fork-tender; drain. Coat a cast-iron skillet with melted butter. Place potatoes in skillet; arrange uncooked bacon slices on top. Bake, covered, at 425 degrees for 25 minutes. Serves 6 to 8.

*Patricia Tilley*
*Sabine, WV*

# Bensons' Ultimate Pancakes

1½ c. all-purpose flour
1 T. baking powder
1 T. sugar
1 t. salt
1¼ c. milk
1 egg yolk, beaten
3 T. butter, melted

1 T. vanilla extract
2 egg whites
1½ to 2 c. blueberries
Garnish: butter, maple syrup,
    whipped cream and
    blueberries

Combine first 8 ingredients in a large bowl. Beat egg whites with an electric mixer at high speed until stiff peaks form. Gently fold into batter. Pour batter by ⅓ cupfuls onto a greased hot griddle. Spoon several blueberries on top of just-poured batter. Cook until bubbles appear on the surface; flip and continue cooking for 2 to 3 more minutes, until golden. Garnish as desired. Makes about one dozen.

*Triann Benson*
*Plano, TX*

## berry sweet too!

Top pancakes with something other than syrup…spoonfuls of fruity jam or homemade preserves, fresh berries and a dusting of powdered sugar or a drizzle of honey are all scrumptious.

# Nutty Maple Waffles

*Crunchy pecans paired with maple...a great way to begin the day! Top with plenty of butter and rich maple syrup.*

1½ c. all-purpose flour
2 T. sugar
1 t. baking powder
¼ t. salt
2 eggs, separated

12-oz. can evaporated milk
3 T. oil
½ t. maple extract
½ c. pecans, finely chopped

Combine flour, sugar, baking powder and salt in a medium bowl; mix well and set aside. Combine egg yolks, evaporated milk, oil and maple extract in a large bowl; blend well. Gradually add flour mixture, beating well after each addition; set aside. Beat egg whites in a small bowl at high speed with an electric mixer until stiff peaks form; fold into batter. For each waffle, pour ½ cup batter onto a preheated, greased waffle iron; sprinkle with one tablespoon nuts. Cook according to manufacturer's instructions. Serves 8.

*Vickie*
*Gooseberry Patch*

# The Best French Toast

8-oz. pkg. cream cheese, softened
8-oz. pkg. frozen mixed berries, thawed
3 T. powdered sugar
1 loaf country-style bread, thickly sliced

1 pt. favorite-flavor ice cream, softened
8 eggs, beaten
2 T. butter
maple syrup

Blend cream cheese, berries and powdered sugar; set aside. Carefully make a pocket in each slice of bread with a knife. Spoon cream cheese mixture into pockets; chill until firm. Stir together ice cream and eggs. Place stuffed bread in egg mixture, turning to coat. Melt butter in a large skillet over medium heat. Add stuffed bread; fry on both sides until golden. Serve with syrup. Serves 8.

Nutty Maple Waffles

# Creamy Cinnamon Rolls

*These delectable bites make a great breakfast treat anytime. You can even make the dough ahead of time. Just place rolls in the pan, cover with greased plastic wrap, refrigerate overnight and let them rise the following morning until double in bulk, approximately two hours.*

16-oz. pkg. frozen white bread
    dough, thawed
2 T. butter, melted
⅔ c. brown sugar, packed
½ c. chopped nuts

1 t. cinnamon
½ c. whipping cream
⅔ c. powdered sugar
1 T. milk

Roll dough into an 18-inch by 6-inch rectangle on a lightly floured surface. Brush with melted butter. Combine brown sugar, nuts and cinnamon. Sprinkle evenly over dough. Roll up jelly-roll style, starting with a long side. Cut into 20 slices; arrange cut-side down in a greased 13"x9" baking pan. Cover and let rise until almost double in bulk, about 1½ hours. Uncover and pour cream over rolls. Bake at 350 degrees for 25 to 30 minutes. Mix together powdered sugar and milk; drizzle over warm rolls. Makes 20.

*Sheila Plock*
*Boalsburg, PA*

# Esther's Delicious Breakfast Treat

*These goodies freeze well. Wrap them in aluminum foil...then just reheat in a warm oven for a quick breakfast.*

1 c. brown sugar, packed
½ to ¾ c. chopped nuts
⅓ c. maple syrup
6 T. butter, softened and divided
8-oz. pkg. cream cheese,
    softened

¼ c. powdered sugar
2 10-oz. tubes refrigerated
    biscuits

Combine brown sugar, nuts, syrup and 4 tablespoons butter in an ungreased 13"x9" baking pan; set aside. Beat cream cheese, powdered sugar and remaining butter with an electric mixer at medium speed until smooth; set aside. Press biscuits into 4-inch circles; spoon one tablespoon cream cheese mixture onto the center of each. Fold dough over cream cheese, forming finger-shaped rolls. Arrange rolls in 2 rows, seam-side down, over brown sugar mixture in pan. Bake at 350 degrees for 20 to 30 minutes, until golden. Let cool for several minutes; turn out onto a serving plate. Serves 8 to 10.

*Esther Goodner*
*Danville, IL*

## easy fruity topping

Stir ¼ cup of your favorite jam into an 8-ounce container of whipped cream cheese. So yummy on toasted bagels!

# Cherry Streusel Coffee Cake

*This easy-to-assemble coffee cake recipe won "Best of Show" several years ago at a county fair and it's been requested at many social events.*

18½-oz. pkg. yellow cake mix, divided
1 env. active dry yeast
1 c. all-purpose flour
2 eggs, beaten

⅔ c. warm water
5 T. butter, melted
21-oz. can cherry pie filling
2 T. sugar
Garnish: chopped nuts

Combine 1½ cups dry cake mix, yeast, flour, eggs and warm water (110 to 115 degrees); stir for 2 minutes. Spread in a lightly greased 13"x9" baking pan. Blend melted butter and remaining cake mix; set aside. Spoon pie filling over batter in pan. Crumble butter mixture over pie filling. Sprinkle sugar over top. Bake at 375 degrees for 30 minutes. Let cool. Drizzle Glaze over cooled cake; sprinkle nuts on top. Serves 15.

## Glaze:

1 c. powdered sugar
1 T. corn syrup

1 to 2 T. water

Combine powdered sugar and corn syrup. Stir in enough water to form a glaze consistency.

*Joyceann Dreibellis*
*Wooster, OH*

Apple Pie Oatmeal

# Apple Pie Oatmeal

*This is an easy, healthy and hearty breakfast.*

1 c. water
½ c. long-cooking oats,
    uncooked
⅛ t. salt

2 t. brown sugar, packed
1 T. apple, peeled and diced
⅛ t. apple pie spice
Optional: milk or cream

Combine water, oats and salt in a microwave-safe bowl. Cover tightly with plastic wrap, folding back a small edge to allow steam to escape. Microwave on high for 2½ minutes. Stir well. Top with remaining ingredients and milk or cream, if desired. Serves one.

*Jill Ball*
*Highland, UT*


# Best-Ever Breakfast Bars

1 c. granola
1 c. quick-cooking oats,
    uncooked
½ c. all-purpose flour
¼ c. brown sugar, packed
⅛ t. cinnamon
1 c. nuts, coarsely chopped

½ c. dried fruit, chopped into
    small pieces
2 T. ground whole flaxseed meal
⅓ c. canola oil
⅓ c. honey
½ t. vanilla extract
1 egg, beaten

Combine granola and next 7 ingredients in a large bowl. Whisk together oil, honey and vanilla; stir into granola mixture. Add egg; stir to blend. Press mixture into a parchment paper-lined 8"x8" baking pan. Bake at 325 degrees for 30 to 35 minutes, until lightly golden around the edges. Remove from oven and cool 30 minutes to one hour. Slice into bars. Serves 8 to 12.

*Mary Ann Lewis*
*Olive Branch, MS*

If your family doesn't like nuts, use chocolate chips or coconut instead.
For the dried fruit, try raisins, apples, cherries, pineapple, mango or a combination.

# Jill's Banana Butter

*Pumpkin pie spice makes this a great fall breakfast butter...spread it on toast, English muffins or bagels.*

4 ripe bananas, sliced
3 T. lemon juice

1½ c. sugar
1 t. pumpkin pie spice

Place bananas and lemon juice in a food processor; pulse until smooth. Transfer mixture to a saucepan and stir in remaining ingredients. Bring to a boil over medium-high heat. Reduce heat and simmer 15 minutes; stir often. Spoon into an airtight container; cover and keep refrigerated. Makes 3 cups.

*Jill Ball*
*Highland, UT*

## special touch

A pint-size Mason jar filled with homemade fruit butter or sweet spread makes a delightful (and yummy) gift to share with co-workers or neighbors. Use a bit of jute or raffia to tie on a pretty spreader.

# Orange Blossom Honey Butter

½ c. butter, softened          1 T. orange zest
2 T. honey

Beat butter in a small bowl until light and fluffy. Beat in honey and orange zest until well blended. Cover and refrigerate. Makes ½ cup.

*Sharon Demers*
*Dolores, CO*

# Homemade Buttery Syrup

2 c. sugar                    3 T. butter
1 c. evaporated milk          1 t. vanilla extract

Combine sugar and evaporated milk in a saucepan over medium heat. Bring to a boil; reduce heat to low and simmer 10 minutes. Watch carefully to avoid scorching. Remove from heat; add butter and vanilla. Serve warm. Store in refrigerator up to 2 weeks. Makes about 3 cups.

*Susan Matlock*
*Mansfield, MO*

Nutty Banana Shake

# Nutty Banana Shake

*A tasty way to use ripe bananas. Bananas will ripen quickly if placed overnight in a brown paper bag.*

2 to 3 bananas, peeled and
    frozen
1 c. milk

2 T. peanut butter
1 T. honey

Slice frozen bananas and place in a blender with remaining ingredients. Blend until smooth and thick. Serves one.

*Marsha Overholser*
*Ash Grove, MO*


# Just Peachy Coconut Smoothie

*The natural sweetness from the peaches and honey is divine!*

16-oz. pkg. frozen peaches,
    divided
14-oz. can coconut milk

2 T. unsweetened flaked coconut
2 T. honey
1 t. vanilla extract

Place half the peaches in a blender; reserve remaining peaches for another recipe. Add remaining ingredients to blender; process until smooth and creamy, about 30 seconds. If consistency is too thin, add a few extra frozen peaches to thicken. Serves 2.

*Jessica Phillips*
*Bloomington, IN*

Chinese Chicken Spread

# gather with friends

Whether you're preparing for an intimate setting or a large gathering, we have what you're looking for. Claudia's Famous Wing Dip (page 44) blends the flavors of chicken and blue cheese dressing all in one hot and creamy dip. The best part...no messy fingers! For a unique twist, serve Italian Egg Rolls (page 55) with warm pizza sauce. For a thirst-quenching beverage, impress your guests with spicy Old-Fashioned Ginger Beer (page 79). Whatever the occasion, invite loved ones over for a good time and great food.

# Claudia's Famous Wing Dip

You'll need to make a triple batch for tailgating...that's how good this is!

8-oz. pkg. cream cheese, softened
16-oz. container sour cream
1 c. blue cheese salad dressing
½ c. hot wing sauce

2½ c. cooked chicken, shredded
1 c. provolone cheese, shredded
tortilla chips, celery sticks

Beat together cream cheese, sour cream, blue cheese dressing and hot wing sauce in a large bowl until well blended. Stir in chicken and cheese. Pour chicken mixture into a lightly greased 2-quart casserole dish. Cover and bake at 350 degrees for 25 to 30 minutes, until hot and bubbly. Serve warm with tortilla chips and celery sticks for dipping. Makes 6½ cups.

*Jason Keller*
*Carrollton, GA*

# 4-Layer Mexican Dip

*Guests will also welcome fresh veggie dippers such as baby carrots, celery stalks and broccoli flowerets.*

8-oz. pkg. cream cheese, softened
15-oz. can chili with beans
16-oz. jar salsa

8-oz. pkg. shredded Mexican-blend cheese
tortilla chips or crackers

Spread cream cheese into the bottom of an ungreased, microwave-safe 11"x7" glass casserole dish. Layer chili, salsa and cheese on top. Microwave on high for 5 to 7 minutes, until hot and bubbly and cheeses are melted. Serve warm with tortilla chips or crackers for dipping. Serves 4 to 6.

*Sharon Taylor*
*Angelica, NY*

## the big chill

When you need to chill lots of juice boxes, bottled water, cartons of milk or cans of soda, you'll find they chill more quickly on ice than in the refrigerator. Just add beverages to an ice-filled cooler or galvanized tub... you'll save valuable refrigerator space too!

# Salmon Loaf Dip

1 large loaf crusty bread
1 onion, finely chopped
1 to 2 t. oil
8-oz. pkg. cream cheese, softened
2 7¾-oz. cans salmon, drained

3 to 4 T. sour cream
1 t. hot pepper sauce
⅛ t. salt
⅛ t. pepper
1 t. fresh dill weed, chopped

Slice the top from bread loaf. Hollow out center and cut bread into cubes, if desired; set aside. Sauté onion in oil in a medium saucepan over medium heat until tender. Place onion and remaining ingredients in a medium bowl; mix well. Spoon mixture into hollow loaf; replace bread lid and place on an ungreased baking sheet. Bake at 350 degrees for 30 minutes. Add reserved bread cubes to baking sheet, bake both for 3 to 5 more minutes. Serve dip with warmed bread cubes. Serves 4 to 8.

*Suzanne Morley*
*Kent, England*

## set a pretty table

Invite friends over for lunch. Bring out your favorite collections, vintage tablecloths and napkins and mismatched silver and glassware in pretty colors for a festive table setting.

# Texas Cowboy Caviar

16-oz. can black-eyed peas,
    drained and rinsed
16-oz. can pinto beans, drained
    and rinsed
16-oz. can black beans, drained
    and rinsed
15-oz. can shoepeg corn, drained
1 onion, chopped

1 c. celery, chopped
1 c. green pepper, chopped
Optional: 4-oz. jar pimentos,
    drained
1 c. oil
1 c. vinegar
1 c. sugar
corn chips

Combine beans, corn, onion, celery, pepper and pimentos, if desired, in a serving bowl. Whisk together oil, vinegar and sugar in a saucepan and heat to a boil. Cook until thickened. Remove from heat; cool to room temperature. Drizzle oil mixture over vegetable mixture and toss to mix. Cover and refrigerate at least one hour to overnight; drain excess liquid before serving. Serve with corn chips. Serves 15.

*Donna Anderson*
*McHenry, IL*

# Julie's Fresh Guacamole

6 avocados, halved and pitted
3 T. lime juice
½ yellow onion, finely chopped
4 roma tomatoes, chopped
¾ c. sour cream
1 T. ranch salad dressing

1 T. salt or to taste
1 T. pepper or to taste
1 T. chili powder
½ t. cayenne pepper
Garnish: fresh cilantro sprigs
tortilla chips

This recipe is much
more delicious
than store-bought
guacamole, and it's so
simple to make.

Scoop out avocado into a large bowl; mash with a fork. Add lime juice, onion and tomatoes; mix with a spoon. Add sour cream, ranch dressing and seasonings; mix well. Cover with plastic wrap; refrigerate for at least 30 minutes. Garnish with cilantro. Serve with tortilla chips. Serves 8 to 10.

*Julie Dos Santos*
*Fort Pierce, FL*

## fun project for kids

Grow a windowsill garden. Fill an empty jar with water and then use toothpicks to suspend a fresh avocado pit in the water. Place the jar in a sunny window...the new plant will form roots and leaves in just a few days.

Hot Ham & Cheddar Dip

# Hot Ham & Cheddar Dip

1 lb. cooked ham, diced
2 8-oz. pkgs. cream cheese,
   softened
3 c. shredded Cheddar
   cheese, divided
1 onion, diced
1 t. garlic salt
tortilla chips, crackers

Blend together all ingredients except chips, reserving ¼ cup Cheddar cheese for topping. Spread ham mixture in a lightly greased 2-quart casserole dish; sprinkle with remaining cheese. Bake at 350 degrees for 20 minutes, or until warmed through and cheese is melted. Serve with tortilla chips and crackers. Makes 4 cups.

*Jessica Branch*
*Colchester, IL*

If your party is at home, place a variety of dips with an assortment of vegetables, crackers or chips in different areas of the house so that they won't take up valuable space on your buffet table.

# Chinese Chicken Spread
(pictured on page 42)

*Look for the rice crackers in the Asian food section of your grocery store.*

8-oz. pkg. cream cheese, softened
1¾ c. cooked chicken breast,
   shredded
½ c. carrot, peeled and grated
½ c. slivered almonds
1 clove garlic, minced
3 T. green onions, sliced
3 T. soy sauce
½ t. ground ginger
Garnish: sweet-and-sour sauce,
   corn tortilla chips or
   teriyaki-flavored rice crackers

Spread softened cream cheese onto a platter. Mix next 7 ingredients in a bowl; spread over top of cream cheese layer. Drizzle with sauce. Serve with chips or rice crackers around edge of platter. Serves 8.

*Lisa Colombo*
*Appleton, WI*

# Brown Sugar Fruit Dip

8 oz. pkg. cream cheese, softened
½ c. brown sugar, packed
1 c. sour cream
1 t. vanilla extract
1 c. frozen whipped topping, thawed
gingersnap cookies or assorted fruit slices

In a bowl, beat cream cheese and brown sugar with an electric mixer at medium speed. Add sour cream and vanilla; beat until blended and smooth. Fold in whipped topping. Cover and chill for at least 4 hours before serving. Serve with gingersnaps or fruit. Serves 8 to 10.

*Kathy Harris*
*Valley Center, KS*

Italian Egg Rolls

# Italian Egg Rolls

½ c. onion, chopped
½ c. green pepper, chopped
2 t. oil
1 lb. ground sweet or hot Italian
    pork sausage
2 10-oz. pkgs. frozen chopped
    spinach, thawed and drained

3 c. shredded mozzarella cheese
½ c. grated Parmesan cheese
½ t. garlic powder
14-oz. pkg. egg roll wrappers
olive oil for deep frying
pizza sauce, warmed

Sauté onion and green pepper in oil in a skillet over medium heat. Place onion mixture in a medium bowl and set aside. Brown sausage in skillet; drain and combine with onion mixture. Add spinach, cheeses and garlic powder; mix well. Top each egg roll wrapper with 3 table-spoons of mixture; roll up, following directions on egg roll package. Heat 3 to 4 inches oil in a deep fryer. Fry egg rolls, in batches, until golden. Drain on paper towels. Serve warm with pizza sauce for dipping. Makes 8.

*Carolyn Scilanbro*
*Hampton, VA*

# Ranch Ham & Tortilla Pinwheels

1 c. deli smoked ham, cubed
2 8-oz. pkgs. cream cheese,
    softened
0.4-oz. pkg. ranch salad dressing
    mix

2 green onions, minced
14 12-inch flour tortillas
4-oz. can diced green chiles
Optional: 2¼-oz. can sliced
    black olives, drained

Mix together ham, cream cheese, ranch dressing mix and green onions in a bowl; spread on tortillas. Sprinkle with chiles and olives, if desired. Roll tortillas tightly. Chill 2 hours or up to 24 hours. Slice rolls into one-inch pieces. Makes 3 dozen.

# Quilters' Squares

1 lb. ground beef
1 lb. ground pork sausage
1 onion, chopped
16-oz. pkg. pasteurized process
    cheese spread, cubed

1 T. Worcestershire sauce
½ t. garlic salt
½ t. dried oregano
2 T. fresh parsley, minced
1 loaf sliced party rye

Brown beef, pork and onion in a skillet over medium heat; drain.
Add remaining ingredients except rye slices to skillet. Cook and stir
until cheese is melted. Arrange rye slices on an ungreased baking
sheet. Spread each rye slice with one tablespoon beef mixture. Bake at
450 degrees for 8 minutes, or until bubbly. Makes 3 dozen.

*Dolores Brock*
*Wellton, AZ*


# Mexican Nacho Chips

*Try the hamburger mixture as an easy meal...just spoon it over bite-size
tortilla chips and garnish it with your favorite taco toppings.*

2 lbs. ground beef
1 onion, finely chopped
16-oz. jar salsa
15-oz. can black beans, drained
    and rinsed
15-oz. can corn, drained

15-oz. can diced tomatoes with
    green chiles
1¼-oz. pkg. taco seasoning mix
13-oz. pkg. large scoop-type
    tortilla chips

Brown ground beef with onion in a large skillet over medium heat;
drain. Stir in remaining ingredients except chips. Mix well until heated
through. Place a spoonful of mixture into each tortilla chip and serve
immediately. Serves 10 to 12.

*Jena Buckler*
*Bloomington Springs, TN*

# Chutney-Topped Brie

2 T. chopped almonds or walnuts
8-oz. round Brie cheese

¼ c. apricot or cranberry chutney
assorted crackers

Toast nuts in a small non-stick skillet over medium-low heat, stirring often, for 2 to 3 minutes. Set aside. Trim and discard rind from top of Brie round, leaving a ¼-inch border. Place Brie in an ungreased oven-proof serving dish; top with chutney. Bake, uncovered, at 400 degrees for 10 minutes, or until slightly melted; watch closely. Sprinkle nuts over Brie. Serve warm with assorted crackers. Serves 8 to 10.

*Kathy Harris*
*Valley Center, KS*

## choose carefully

Underripe Brie will feel hard when gently pressed with your finger. If it feels too runny, it's probably overripe. Once ripened, it should be used within a few days. Purchase Brie rounds no more than one-inch thick that have a slightly sweet aroma.

# The Best-Yet Buffalo Wings

*These wings are sweet, but the sauce is hot!*

3 lbs. chicken wings
seasoned salt to taste
2-oz. bottle hot pepper sauce

1 c. brown sugar, packed
1 c. water
1 T. mustard seed

Arrange chicken wings on a lightly greased 15"x10" jelly-roll pan. Sprinkle with seasoned salt. Bake at 400 degrees for 20 minutes; turn wings. Bake for 20 to 30 more minutes, until golden and juices run clear when chicken is pierced with a fork; drain. Arrange on serving platter. Combine remaining ingredients in a saucepan; bring to a boil over medium heat. Reduce heat to low; cook until mixture caramelizes and becomes a dark burgundy color, stirring occasionally. Pour sauce over wings before serving, or serve on the side for dipping. Makes about 3 dozen.

*Kristen Taylor*
*Fort Smith, AR*

## clean hands

A tray of warm, moistened towels is a must when serving sticky barbecue ribs or chicken wings! Dampen fingertip towels in water and a dash of lemon juice, roll up and microwave on high for 10 to 15 seconds.

# Slow-Cooker Honey-BBQ Chicken Wings

*Add a side of steamed rice and veggies for a tasty no-fuss meal.*

3 lbs. chicken wings
salt and pepper to taste
1 c. honey
¼ c. barbecue sauce

¼ c. teriyaki sauce
¼ c. soy sauce
2 T. oil
1 clove garlic, minced

Arrange chicken wings on a lightly greased broiler pan; sprinkle with salt and pepper. Broil for 12 to 15 minutes on each side, until golden. Transfer wings to a slow cooker. Combine remaining ingredients and pour over wings. Cover and cook on high setting 2 hours or on low setting for 4 hours. Serves 4 to 6.

*Kendall Hale*
*Lynn, MA*

# Crispy Chicken Tasties

*These delicious appetizers can be served at family dinners or for snacking while watching sports on television. They're even good cold!*

½ c. lemon juice
3 T. soy sauce
½ t. salt
3 lbs. boneless, skinless chicken breasts, cut into one-inch cubes

1 c. all-purpose flour
1 T. paprika
1 T. pepper
½ t. salt
peanut oil for frying

Mix lemon juice, soy sauce and salt together in a large bowl. Add chicken. Refrigerate for 3 hours, stirring occasionally. Drain, discarding marinade. Combine flour and seasonings in a separate bowl. Coat chicken in flour mixture. Heat oil in a large skillet over medium-high heat. Add chicken; cook until golden on all sides and juices run clear when chicken is pierced with a fork. Drain on paper towels before serving. Serves 6 to 8.

*Kelly Korokis*
*Fredericktown, MO*

## back in the day

An old-fashioned picnic lunch used to be a terrific way to relax on a sunny afternoon. Relive some of those memories and pack sandwiches along with fresh fruits and veggies in vintage tins for easy toting. Along with some ice-cold lemonade, what could be better?

# Pork & Apple Meatballs

*Serve these yummy meatballs immediately or keep warm in a slow cooker until ready to serve.*

Keep your hands moist with cool water when shaping meatballs so that they won't be so sticky. Use a small ice cream scoop to form them so that your meatballs will be the same size and cook evenly.

1 lb. ground pork sausage
1¼ c. pork-flavored stuffing mix
½ c. low-sodium chicken broth
½ c. Honeycrisp apple, cored, peeled and diced
½ c. onion, diced

1 egg, beaten
1½ t. mustard
½ c. shredded sharp Cheddar cheese
Optional: barbecue sauce

Combine all ingredients except barbecue sauce in a large bowl. Form into balls by tablespoonfuls. Place on a lightly greased 15"x10" jelly-roll pan. Bake at 350 degrees for 18 to 20 minutes, until meatballs are no longer pink in the middle. Brush with barbecue sauce, if desired. Serves 8 to 10.

*Emmaline Dunkley*
*Pine City, MN*

# Sun-Dried Tomato Toasties

½ c. sun-dried tomato and olive relish
2¼-oz. can chopped black olives, drained

2 t. garlic, chopped
8-oz. pkg. shredded mozzarella cheese, divided
1 loaf French bread, thinly sliced

Mix together relish, olives, garlic and ¼ cup cheese; spread evenly on bread slices. Arrange bread on an ungreased baking sheet; sprinkle bread with remaining cheese. Bake at 300 degrees for 4 to 5 minutes, until cheese melts; serve immediately. Makes 2 to 3 dozen.

*Lisanne Miller*
*Canton, MS*

Pork & Apple Meatballs

# Crabmeat-Stuffed Eggs

1 doz. eggs, hard-boiled, peeled
    and halved
1 c. crabmeat, flaked
1 c. celery, finely chopped
2 T. green pepper, finely chopped
⅛ c. sour cream
1 T. mayonnaise-type salad
    dressing
Garnish: thin green pepper slice

Scoop egg yolks into a bowl and mash with fork. Place egg whites on a serving dish and set aside. Combine mashed yolks and remaining ingredients except garnish; blend well. Spoon mixture into egg whites. Chill until serving time. Garnish, if desired. Makes 2 dozen.

*Marilyn Miller*
*Fort Washington, PA*

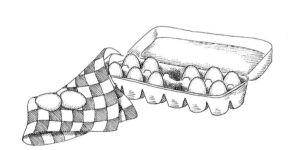

## handy tip

In need of a large batch of deviled eggs for a party or picnic? Whip 'em up in no time by spooning the egg yolk filling into a plastic zipping bag. Snip off a corner and pipe the filling into the egg white halves...simple!

# Dad's Chili-Cheese Ball

16-oz. pkg. pasteurized process
    cheese spread, diced and
    softened
8-oz. pkg. cream cheese, softened

½ t. garlic powder
2 to 3 T. chili powder
assorted crackers

Combine first 3 ingredients in a medium bowl; mix well and form into a ball. Pour chili powder onto a plate. Roll cheese ball in chili powder until completely coated. Wrap in plastic wrap. Keep refrigerated up to 2 days before serving. Serve with assorted crackers. Serves 8 to 10.

*Holly Child*
*Parker, CO*

## ready-set-go snacks!

When you need a little something extra for guests but time is short, just pick up a few nibblers at the store. Assorted olives, fancy nuts, cream cheese and crackers, cubed cheese and shrimp cocktail all make quick & easy treats.

# Savory Sausage Balls

8-oz. pkg. ground pork sausage
¼ c. onion, finely chopped
14½-oz. jar sauerkraut, drained
    and chopped
1 c. plus 2 T. dry bread crumbs,
    divided
3-oz. pkg. cream cheese, softened
2 T. dried parsley
⅛ t. garlic salt
¼ t. pepper
1 t. mustard
2 eggs, beaten
¼ c. milk
¼ c. all-purpose flour
oil for frying

*These delectable treats are a great make-ahead appetizer too...assemble and fry them ahead of time and then freeze until you are ready to bake them.*

Brown sausage in a skillet over medium heat; drain. Add onion, sauerkraut and 2 tablespoons bread crumbs to skillet; mix well. Blend together cream cheese, seasonings and mustard in a small bowl. Add to skillet and stir until well blended. Place mixture into a large bowl; chill one hour. In a bowl, whisk together eggs and milk. Mix flour and remaining bread crumbs in a shallow plate. Roll sausage mixture into one-inch balls. Dip in egg mixture and roll in bread crumb mixture. Fry balls in hot oil, in batches, until golden on all sides; drain. Bake, uncovered, at 375 degrees in an ungreased 9"x9" baking pan for 20 minutes. Makes about 2 dozen.

*Lori Hoffman*
*Gibsonia, PA*

# Celebration Fruit Salsa

1 orange, peeled and finely
    chopped
2 kiwi, peeled and finely chopped
1 jalapeño pepper, seeded and
    chopped
½ fresh pineapple, peeled and
    finely chopped, or 8-oz. can
    crushed pineapple, drained

1 c. strawberries, hulled and
    chopped
¼ c. green or yellow pepper,
    finely chopped
¼ c. green onions, thinly sliced
1 T. lime or lemon juice
Garnish: kiwi slices
tortilla chips

Combine all ingredients except garnish and chips in a large bowl; stir well. Chill 2 hours or up to 24 hours. Garnish, if desired. Serve with tortilla chips. Makes 3 cups.

*Lavonda Wingfield*
*Boaz, AL*

# Seeded Tortilla Crisps

*Bake up these spicy strips in a jiffy! They're a pleasing change from ordinary chips...serve with spreads, salads and soups.*

¼ c. butter, melted
8 10-inch flour tortillas
¾ c. grated Parmesan cheese
1 egg white, beaten

Garnish: sesame, poppy and/or
    caraway seed
onion powder, cayenne pepper
    or ground cumin to taste

Brush butter lightly over one side of each tortilla; sprinkle evenly with cheese and press down lightly. Carefully turn tortillas over. Brush other side with egg white and sprinkle with desired seeds and seasonings. Cut each tortilla into 4 strips with a pastry cutter or knife. Place strips, cheese-side down, on a lightly greased baking sheet. Bake at 400 degrees, on middle rack of oven, for 8 to 10 minutes, until crisp and golden. Cool on a wire rack. Makes about 2½ dozen.

*Jewel Grindley*
*Lindenhurst, IL*

Celebration Fruit Salsa

# Marinated Shrimp Appetizer

*A flavorful appetizer that's simple to prepare for a special gathering.*

2 onions, thinly sliced
1½ c. oil
1½ c. white vinegar
½ c. sugar
¼ c. capers, undrained

1½ t. celery seed
1½ t. salt
2 lbs. medium shrimp, cooked
    and peeled

    Combine all ingredients except shrimp in a large bowl; mix well. Add shrimp; stir to coat well. Cover and refrigerate for 6 hours or up to 24 hours, stirring occasionally. Drain shrimp, discarding marinade. Serves 8 to 10.

*Gail Konschak*
*Millville, NJ*

## perfect every time

Always purchase fresh shrimp if you can. Using frozen shrimp in recipes that require marinating will make them chewy. Frozen shrimp should always be placed in a bowl of water in the refrigerator until completely thawed.

White Chocolate Party Mix

# White Chocolate Party Mix

5 c. doughnut-shaped oat cereal
5 c. bite-size crispy corn cereal
    squares
10-oz. pkg. mini pretzel twists
2 c. salted peanuts
16-oz. pkg. candy-coated
    chocolates
2 12-oz. pkgs. white chocolate
    chips
3 T. oil

Combine first 5 ingredients in a large bowl; set aside. Heat white chocolate chips and oil in a microwave-safe bowl on medium-high for 2 minutes, stirring once. Continue to microwave on high at 30-second intervals; stir until smooth. Pour over cereal mixture and stir well to coat. Spread onto 3 wax paper-lined baking sheets to cool completely. Break apart when cool. Store in an airtight container. Makes 5 quarts.

*Lecia Stevenson*
*Timberville, VA*

# Chili-Lime Pecans

2 T. lime juice
1 T. olive oil
1 t. paprika
1 t. sea salt
1 t. chili powder
½ t. cayenne pepper
3 c. pecan halves

Stir together all ingredients except pecans in a medium bowl. Add pecans and toss to coat well. Spread pecans on an aluminum foil-lined, lightly greased 15"x10" jelly-roll pan. Bake at 350 degrees for 10 to 12 minutes, until pecans are toasted and dry, stirring occasionally. Cool completely; store in an airtight container. Makes 3 cups.

*Sharon Jones*
*Oklahoma City, OK*

# Black Forest Fondue

*Go retro yet classic with this chocolatey fondue!*

¾ c. whipping cream
⅛ t. salt
1 c. milk chocolate chips
1 c. semi-sweet chocolate chips

2½ T. cherry extract
1 T. corn syrup
pound cake cubes, assorted fruit
   cubes and slices

Bring cream and salt to a boil in a saucepan over medium heat. Remove from heat. Add chocolates to saucepan; cover and let stand 3 to 4 minutes. Uncover; whisk until chocolate mixture is smooth. Whisk in extract and corn syrup. Serve immediately with pound cake and fruit. May be kept warm in a slow cooker or fondue pot over low heat; stir often. Serves 10.

*Arlene Smulski*
*Lyons, IL*

# Apple-Cheese Fondue

1 clove garlic, minced
1 c. dry white wine or apple juice
½ lb. Gruyère cheese, shredded
½ lb. Swiss cheese, diced
2 T. cornstarch
⅛ t. nutmeg

⅛ t. pepper
1 French baguette, torn into
   bite-size pieces
2 apples, cored, quartered and
   sliced

Combine all ingredients except bread and apples in a fondue pot or medium saucepan over medium heat. Bring to a simmer, stirring constantly, until cheese is melted. Serve with baguette and apple slices for dipping. Serves 4.

*Weda Mosellie*
*Phillipsburg, NJ*

Black Forest Fondue

Rosemary-Lemon-Pineapple
Punch

# Rosemary-Lemon-Pineapple Punch

*A refreshing beverage that's perfect for a garden party or reception.*

46-oz. can unsweetened
   pineapple juice
1½ c. lemon juice
2 c. water
¾ to 1 c. sugar

4 to 5 sprigs fresh rosemary
1-ltr. bottle ginger ale, chilled
Garnish: fresh pineapple slices,
   fresh rosemary sprigs

Combine juices, water, sugar and rosemary in a large saucepan over medium heat. Bring to a boil. Stir until sugar dissolves. Remove from heat; cover and let stand for 15 minutes. Discard rosemary; chill. Before serving, add ginger ale; serve immediately. Garnish, if desired. Serves 12.

*Helene Hamilton*
*Hickory, NC*

# Summer Sparkle

*Having a fancy party? Serve this punch in tall fluted glasses with lots of ice...oh-so refreshing!*

48-oz. bottle ruby red grapefruit
   juice
12-oz. can frozen orange juice
   concentrate, thawed
6-oz. can frozen lemonade
   concentrate, thawed

2-ltr. bottle lemon-lime soda,
   chilled
Optional: lemon slices, fresh
   mint sprigs

For extra-shiny glasses, add a splash of vinegar to the final rinse water either in the dishwater or the sink.

Stir together grapefruit juice, orange juice concentrate and lemonade concentrate in a gallon pitcher; refrigerate until chilled. At serving time, stir in soda; garnish as desired. Serves 16 to 20.

*Eleanor Bamford*
*Boonton, NJ*

# Old-Fashioned Ginger Beer

4 lemons
1 orange
¾ c. fresh ginger, peeled and
    coarsely chopped
¾ c. sugar
¾ c. honey

2 c. boiling water
1¼ c. orange juice
4 c. sparkling mineral water,
    chilled
crushed ice
Garnish: orange slices

Grate 2 tablespoons of zest from lemons and orange. Set orange and one lemon aside. Squeeze ⅓ cup lemon juice from remaining 3 lemons. Set aside. Pulse ginger, sugar and honey in a food processor just until combined; spoon into a pitcher. Add orange and lemon zests and boiling water; stir until sugar dissolves. Cool to room temperature. Stir in orange juice. Cover and refrigerate for at least 24 hours and up to 5 days. Strain before serving. Thinly slice remaining lemon and orange; add to pitcher. Stir in sparkling water. Serve over ice. Garnish, if desired. Serves 8 to 10.

*Amy Butcher*
*Columbus, GA*

## make your own

Try making homemade root beer...it's oh-so easy and delicious! Add 5 gallons of cool water and a 4-pound bag of sugar to a large beverage cooler; stir to dissolve sugar. Blend in a 2-ounce bottle of root beer concentrate. Wearing gloves, slowly add 5 pounds of dry ice to the mixture; cover loosely with lid to allow mixture to bubble. When bubbling is complete, your root beer is ready to enjoy!

Iowa's Best Corn Chowder

# best soups & sandwiches

When a chill is in the air, what could be better than a filling sandwich and a bowl of hot soup? Chock-full of meat and vegetables, Hobo Stew (page 85) paired with Carol's Veggie Panini (page 110) makes for a hearty weeknight meal. Delicately seasoned and full of nutritious goodness, Hearty, Healthy Chicken Salad (page 104) is perfect with a bag of baked chips and a beverage. Mix and match these mouthwatering recipes as a combo or serve them on their own.

# Erma Lee's Chicken Soup

*My family still requests this soup at the first sign of cold weather.*

*—Shirley*

3 14-oz. cans chicken broth
⅔ c. onion, diced
⅔ c. carrot, peeled and diced
⅔ c. celery, diced
2 10¾-oz. cans cream of
    mushroom soup

4 boneless, skinless chicken
    breasts, cooked and chopped
8-oz. pkg. pasteurized process
    cheese spread, cubed
1 c. shredded Cheddar cheese
1 c. cooked rice

Bring broth to a boil in a stockpot over medium heat. Add vegetables; cook until tender, about 10 minutes. Stir in remaining ingredients; simmer over low heat until cheeses melt and soup is heated through, about 15 minutes. Serves 4 to 6.

*Shirley White*
*Gatesville, TX*

# Santa Fe Spicy Chicken Soup

1 boneless, skinless chicken
    breast, cubed
2 to 3 potatoes, peeled and cubed
14½-oz. can diced tomatoes
    with green chiles

14-oz. can chicken broth
1¼-oz. pkg. taco seasoning mix

Combine all ingredients in an ungreased microwave-safe one-quart casserole dish. Mix well; cover tightly with plastic wrap. Microwave on high for 13 to 16 minutes, until chicken is cooked and potatoes are tender. Let stand for 2 minutes before removing from microwave. Remove plastic wrap carefully. Serves 4.

*Kathie Jester*
*Yadkinville, NC*

Erma Lee's Chicken Soup

# Hobo Stew

1 lb. ground beef
1 onion, diced
1 T. seasoned salt with onion
    & garlic
4 potatoes, peeled and cubed
3 carrots, peeled and sliced
28-oz. can whole tomatoes,
    broken up

15¼-oz. can corn
15-oz. can black beans
14½-oz. can green beans
1.35-oz. pkg. onion soup mix
0.87-oz. pkg. brown gravy mix
1-oz. pkg. ranch salad dressing
    mix

Brown beef with onion and seasoning in a stockpot over medium heat. Drain; add remaining ingredients and enough water to cover. Bring to a boil; reduce heat. Simmer until vegetables are tender, about 30 to 40 minutes, adding a little more water if needed. Serves 8 to 10.

*Char Pletcher*
*Lone Grove, OK*

## cute collectibles

Be on the lookout at flea markets and antiques shops for vintage tin bread boxes. Fill them with a variety of plants for a mini garden patch!

# Jan's Prize-Winning Chili

This recipe won a chili cook-off at my church. Every Halloween I make it in a slow cooker and then set it to warm...that way everyone can eat either before or after trick-or-treating.

—Jan

1½ lbs. ground beef
1 onion, chopped
1 clove garlic, minced
29-oz. can tomato sauce
28-oz. can diced tomatoes
16-oz. can pinto beans, drained and rinsed
16-oz. can red kidney beans, drained and rinsed
7-oz. can diced green chiles
2 cubes beef bouillon
2 1¼-oz. pkgs. chili seasoning mix
Garnish: shredded Cheddar cheese, sour cream, minced onion

Brown beef, onion and garlic in a Dutch oven over medium heat; drain. Mix together remaining ingredients except garnish; add to ground beef mixture. Cover and cook over low heat for at least one hour, stirring occasionally. Top servings with cheese, sour cream and minced onion. Serves 10 to 12.

*Jan Durston*
*Norco, CA*

# Easy Turkey Gumbo

*Looking for a twist on soup made with turkey leftovers? Try this!*

3 c. turkey broth
2 c. cooked turkey, diced
½ c. onion, chopped
¼ c. celery, chopped
¼ c. long-cooking rice,
    uncooked

10-oz. pkg. frozen cut okra
10-oz. can diced tomatoes with
    green chiles
½ t. salt
⅛ t. pepper

Bring broth to a boil in a large saucepan over medium heat. Add remaining ingredients; reduce heat. Cover and simmer for 15 to 20 minutes, until vegetables and rice are tender. Serves 4 to 6.

*Karin Coursin*
*Waynesburg, PA*

## yummy soup topping

Make biscuit toppers for bowls of thick, hearty turkey or chicken soup...they're almost like individual pot pies. Separate jumbo refrigerated biscuits, flatten them and bake according to package directions until golden. Top each soup bowl with a biscuit and dig in!

# Slow-Cooker Chile Verde Soup

½ lb. pork tenderloin, cut into
    ½-inch cubes
1 t. oil
2 c. chicken broth
2 15-oz. cans white beans,
    drained and rinsed

2 4-oz. cans diced green chiles
¼ t. ground cumin
¼ t. dried oregano
salt and pepper to taste
Optional: chopped fresh cilantro

Cook pork in oil in a skillet over medium heat for one to 2 minutes
or until browned. Place pork in a 4-quart slow cooker. Add remaining
ingredients except cilantro; stir well. Cover and cook on low setting for
4 to 6 hours. Sprinkle cilantro over each serving, if desired. Serves 6 to 8.

*Lisa Sett*
*Thousand Oaks, CA*

## tasty twist

A fun new way to serve cornbread...mix up the batter,
thin slightly with a little extra milk and then bake until
crisp in a waffle iron. Perfect with your favorite soup
or chili!

# New England Fish Chowder

Garnish chowder with oyster crackers and chopped fresh parsley. Add a little chopped bacon for a more smoky flavor.

1 T. oil
½ c. onion, chopped
2½ c. potato, peeled and diced
1½ c. boiling water
salt and pepper to taste
1 lb. frozen cod or haddock
    fillets, thawed and cut into
    large chunks

2 c. milk
1 T. butter
Garnish: fresh parsley sprig

Heat oil in a large saucepan over medium heat. Add onion; cook until tender. Add potato, water, salt and pepper. Reduce heat; cover and simmer for 15 to 20 minutes, until potatoes are tender. Add fish; simmer until fish flakes easily with a fork, about 5 minutes. Add milk and butter just before serving; heat through. Garnish with fresh parsley sprig. Serves 6.

# Tortellini-Sausage Soup

Your family will love this hearty, savory soup. Pop some garlic bread in the oven and toss a crisp green salad... dinner is served!

1 lb. ground Italian pork sausage
1 c. onion, chopped
2 cloves garlic, minced
4 c. beef broth
½ c. dry red wine or beef broth
28-oz. can crushed tomatoes
28-oz. can diced tomatoes
15-oz. can tomato sauce

1 c. carrot, peeled and chopped
1 T. dried parsley
½ t. dried basil
½ t. dried oregano
1 c. zucchini, chopped
9-oz. pkg. refrigerated cheese
    tortellini, uncooked

Brown sausage in a stockpot over medium heat; drain. Add onion and garlic; sauté until tender. Stir in broth, wine or broth, and next 7 ingredients. Bring to a boil; stir well. Reduce heat; cover and simmer for 30 minutes. Stir in zucchini and tortellini; cover and simmer for 15 more minutes, or until tortellini are heated through. Serves 10 to 12.

New England Fish Chowder

# Pasta e Fagioli

*The name of this mostly meatless Italian dish means pasta and beans. You'll find many variations that use pancetta or prosciutto...we added bacon to our version.*

15-oz. can cannellini beans
2 T. olive oil
3 slices bacon, coarsely chopped
2 stalks celery, chopped
2 carrots, peeled and chopped
1 onion, chopped
2 cloves garlic, minced
3 14½-oz. cans chicken broth
15-oz. can kidney beans,
    drained and rinsed
1 c. small shell pasta, uncooked
salt and pepper to taste
Garnish: 6 T. grated Parmesan
    cheese

Mash undrained cannellini beans with a fork in a bowl and set aside. Heat oil in a large saucepan over medium heat; add bacon and next 4 ingredients. Cook for 7 to 10 minutes, stirring occasionally, until bacon is crisp and vegetables are softened. Add broth, cannellini beans and kidney beans; bring to a boil over high heat. Stir pasta into soup. Reduce heat to medium. Cook, uncovered, for 6 to 8 minutes, stirring frequently, until pasta is tender. Add salt and pepper; top each serving with a tablespoon of cheese. Serves 6.

*Maddie Schaum*
*Mount Airy, MD*

# Caroline's Leek Soup

| | |
|---|---|
| 1 leek, halved lengthwise and sliced | 14½-oz. can chicken broth |
| 1 T. water | 1¼ c. milk |
| 1 t. butter | 1¼ t. salt |
| 1 head cauliflower, cut into 1-inch pieces | ¾ t. coriander |
| | ¼ t. pepper |
| | Garnish: 1 T. sliced almonds |

Rinse leek well in cold water; pat dry. Combine water and butter in a saucepan over medium-high heat. Add leek and cauliflower; cook for 5 minutes, stirring occasionally. Stir in remaining ingredients except garnish and bring to a boil. Reduce heat to low and simmer, covered, for 20 minutes. Transfer soup, in batches, to a blender; purée until smooth. Garnish servings with almonds. Serves 4.

*Laura Fuller*
*Fort Wayne, IN*

## rinse well!

To quickly clean leeks, slice them into 2-inch lengths and soak in a bowl of cold water. Swish them in the water and drain. Refill the bowl and swish again until the water is clear. They're ready to use…simply drain and pat dry.

# Iowa's Best Corn Chowder

(pictured on page 80)

*Iowa is corn country, and this soup is a local favorite.*

½ c. onion, diced

1 clove garlic, minced

½ t. ground cumin

1 t. olive oil

4 c. vegetable broth

4 c. corn

2 new potatoes, diced

½ t. kosher salt

⅛ t. pepper

¾ c. milk

1 t. fresh cilantro, chopped

Sauté onion, garlic and cumin in oil in a stockpot over medium heat for 5 minutes, or until onion is tender. Add broth and next 4 ingredients; bring to a boil. Reduce to a simmer and cook for 20 minutes, or until potatoes are tender. Add milk and cilantro; cook and stir to heat through. Serves 8.

*Kay Marone*
*Des Moines, IA*

## in season is best

The difference between really sweet, tender corn and tough corn is in when it's picked. Ideally you want to pick it, cook it and enjoy it the same day.

Spicy Squash Soup

# Spicy Squash Soup

2 butternut squash, peeled,
   seeded and cubed
1 stalk celery, finely diced
1 jalapeño pepper, seeded and
   finely diced
½ onion, finely diced

2 c. chicken broth
12-oz. can evaporated milk
½ c. brown sugar, packed
½ c. water
salt and pepper to taste
ground cumin to taste

Place squash in a large saucepan and cover with water. Cook over medium-high heat until tender; drain. Mash squash and measure out 4 cups. Return 4 cups squash to saucepan over medium-low heat; stir in remaining ingredients except cumin. Simmer, covered, for 45 minutes. Cool slightly. Purée soup until smooth, adding to a blender in small batches. Return soup to saucepan over low heat just long enough to heat through; stir in cumin. Serves 6 to 8.

*Arden Regnier*
*East Moriches, NY*

*One year we were getting tired of eating leftover Thanksgiving turkey, and I had a lot of leftover squash too. So I came up with this recipe...it's a satisfying supper with a basket of cornbread muffins.*

*—Arden*

# Garden-Fresh Gazpacho

6 to 8 tomatoes, chopped
1 onion, finely chopped
1 to 2 stalks celery, chopped
1 cucumber, peeled and chopped
1 green pepper, chopped
1 clove garlic, finely chopped
4 c. tomato juice

2 T. fresh parsley or cilantro,
   chopped
2 T. lemon juice
salt and pepper to taste
4 drops hot pepper sauce
Optional: sour cream

Combine all ingredients except sour cream in a large container or gallon-size Mason jar. Stir well. Cover and refrigerate until well chilled. Dollop each serving with sour cream, if desired. Serves 12 to 15.

*Patsy Johnson*
*Salem, MO*

*For a twist, swap out the tomatoes for avocados, or try plain yogurt for a yummy white gazpacho.*

# Easy Tomato Soup

*Other tasty additions to try...chopped fresh basil, chopped fresh chives, chopped fresh rosemary, croutons, freshly grated Parmesan cheese and grated lemon zest.*

28-oz. can Italian-seasoned
    diced tomatoes
26-oz. can tomato soup
32-oz. container chicken broth

½ t. pepper
Optional: sour cream, chopped
    fresh basil

Pulse tomatoes in a food processor or blender 3 to 4 times, or until finely diced. Stir together tomatoes, soup, chicken broth and pepper in a Dutch oven. Cook over medium heat, stirring occasionally, for 10 minutes, or until thoroughly heated. Top servings with sour cream and chopped fresh basil, if desired. Makes 11 cups.

## top with cheese toasts

Cut bread with a mini cookie cutter and brush lightly with olive oil. Place on a broiler pan and broil for 2 to 3 minutes or until golden. Turn over and sprinkle with freshly shredded Parmesan cheese. Broil another 2 to 3 minutes, until cheese melts. Top your favorite soup with crunchy cheese toasts.

Dagwood Burgers

# Dagwood Burgers

*Buns taste better toasted and won't get soggy. Lightly butter buns and place on a hot pan or grill for 30 seconds, or until toasted.*

2 lbs. lean ground beef
1 lb. ground Italian pork sausage
2 c. dry bread crumbs
1 onion, chopped
½ c. barbecue sauce
1 egg, beaten

1.35-oz. pkg. onion soup mix
1 t. jalapeño pepper, diced
salt and pepper to taste
12 to 15 hamburger buns, split
Optional: lettuce leaf

Mix first 8 ingredients in a very large bowl. Form into 12 to 15 patties; sprinkle with salt and pepper. Place on a charcoal grill or in a skillet over medium heat. Cook burgers to desired doneness. Serve on buns. Garnish each serving with lettuce leaf, if desired. Makes 12 to 15 burgers.

*Jennifer Scott*
*Checotah, OK*

# Debbie's Savory Roast Sandwiches

3 to 4-lb. beef or pork roast
14-oz. bottle catsup
½ c. taco sauce
1 onion, chopped
2 cloves garlic, pressed
2 T. brown sugar, packed

2 T. Worcestershire sauce
1 T. vinegar
⅛ t. dried oregano
⅛ t. dry mustard
⅛ t. pepper
10 to 12 hard rolls, split

Place roast in a 5 to 6-quart slow cooker. Mix together catsup and remaining ingredients except rolls; pour over roast. Cover and cook on low setting for 5 to 6 hours. Remove roast from slow cooker; shred with 2 forks. Serve on rolls. Makes 10 to 12 sandwiches.

*Debbie Fuls*
*Pennsylvania Furnace, PA*

# Pepper Steak Sammies

1 to 1¼ lbs. beef sirloin or
    ribeye steak
2 green peppers, thinly sliced
1 onion, sliced
4 cloves garlic, minced and
    divided

1 T. oil
salt and pepper to taste
⅓ c. butter, softened
4 French rolls, split and toasted

Grill or broil steak to desired doneness; set aside. Sauté green peppers, onion and 2 cloves garlic in hot oil in a skillet over medium heat until crisp-tender; drain. Slice steak thinly; add to skillet and heat through. Sprinkle with salt and pepper. Blend butter and remaining garlic; spread over cut sides of rolls. Spoon steak mixture onto bottom halves of rolls; cover with tops. Makes 4 sandwiches.

*Vickie*
*Gooseberry Patch*

## bottled vs. fresh

Keep a bottle of minced garlic on hand to save time when you're in a hurry. If swapping for fresh, remember that ½ teaspoon equals one clove.

# Hearty, Healthy Chicken Salad

4 boneless, skinless chicken
    breasts, cooked and diced
½ c. celery, chopped
¼ c. onion, chopped
½ c. sweetened dried
    cranberries

¼ c. sunflower seeds
½ to 1 c. low-fat plain yogurt
1½ t. dried sage
1½ t. poultry seasoning
10 slices favorite bread, toasted

Combine chicken, celery, onion, cranberries and sunflower seeds in a large bowl. Slowly stir in yogurt; mix well. Add seasonings. Serve on toasted bread. Makes 5 sandwiches.

*Heather Cooper*
*Everett, WA*

## check for freshness

Poultry seasoning combines thyme, sage, marjoram, rosemary, pepper and nutmeg. Pick up a fresh jar early in the season...you'll be ready to spice up any savory dish.

# Regina's Stuffed Pitas

*Pitas are a super change from buns. Try them stuffed with any of your favorite sandwich fillings or even a crisp salad.*

½ lb. deli roast beef, cut into
    thin strips
2 c. romaine lettuce, shredded
1 c. carrot, peeled and shredded
1 c. cucumber, thinly sliced
½ c. red onion, thinly sliced

⅓ c. crumbled feta cheese
3 T. pine nuts, toasted
4 pita rounds, halved and split
2 T. mayonnaise
2 T. milk
1 T. cider vinegar

Stir together beef and next 6 ingredients. Spoon mixture evenly inside pita halves. Whisk together remaining ingredients. Lightly drizzle over each pita filling. Makes 4 sandwiches.

*Regina Vining*
*Warwick, RI*


# Caesar Focaccia Sandwich

2 c. mixed salad greens
¼ c. Caesar salad dressing
8-inch round focaccia bread,
    halved horizontally
4 slices Cheddar cheese

¼ lb. deli ham, thinly shaved
¼ lb. deli turkey, thinly shaved
1 tomato, sliced
1 sliced red onion, separated
    into rings

Toss salad greens with salad dressing; set aside. Layer bottom half of focaccia with greens mixture and remaining ingredients. Add top half of focaccia; cut into halves or quarters. Serves 2 to 4.

*Wendy Ball*
*Battle Creek, MI*

# Tangy Turkey Salad Croissants

The day after Thanksgiving, my mom, sisters and I decided we wanted more than just the usual turkey sandwich. We combined some of our favorite flavors and came up with these...we love them.

—Wendy

2 c. cooked turkey breast, cubed
1 orange, peeled and chopped
½ c. cranberries, finely chopped
½ c. mayonnaise
1 t. mustard
1 t. sugar
½ t. salt
¼ c. chopped pecans
6 croissants, split
Garnish: lettuce leaves

Combine turkey, orange, cranberries, mayonnaise, mustard, sugar and salt; chill. Stir in pecans before serving. Top each croissant half with ½ cup turkey mixture and a lettuce leaf. Top with remaining croissant half. Makes 6 sandwiches.

*Wendy Jacobs*
*Idaho Falls, ID*

# Avocado Egg Salad Sandwiches

*A fresh and delicious twist on egg salad...serve it on your favorite hearty bread!*

6 eggs, hard-boiled, peeled and chopped
2 avocados, cubed
½ c. red onion, minced
⅓ c. mayonnaise
3 T. sweet pickles, chopped
1 T. mustard
salt and pepper to taste
12 slices bread

Mash eggs with a fork in a bowl until crumbly. Add remaining ingredients except bread slices. Gently mix together until blended. Spread egg mixture evenly over 6 bread slices. Top with remaining bread slices. Makes 6 sandwiches.

*Crystal Bruns*
*Iliff, CO*

Tangy Turkey Salad Croissants

# Extra-Cheesy Grilled Cheese

*Delicious in winter with a steaming bowl of tomato soup...scrumptious in summer made with produce fresh from the garden!*

¼ c. butter, softened
8 slices sourdough bread
4 slices provolone cheese
4 slices mozzarella cheese

Optional: 4 slices red onion,
  4 slices tomato,
  ¼ c. chopped fresh basil

Spread 1½ teaspoons butter on each of 8 bread slices. Place one bread slice, butter-side down, in a large skillet or on a hot griddle. Layer one slice provolone and one slice mozzarella cheese on bread slice. Top with an onion slice, tomato slice and one tablespoon basil, if desired. Top with a bread slice, butter-side up. Reduce heat to medium-low. Cook until golden on one side, about 3 to 5 minutes; flip and cook until golden on other side. Repeat to cook remaining sandwiches. Makes 4 sandwiches.

## double-duty grill

Your countertop grill can be so versatile...it's also terrific for grilling thick sandwiches to perfection.

# Carol's Veggie Panini

2 T. balsamic vinegar
1 T. olive oil
½ t. salt
⅛ t. pepper
1 eggplant, cut into ¼-inch-thick
　　slices

1 zucchini, cut into 8 slices
1 red pepper, quartered
8 slices ciabatta bread
1 c. shredded mozzarella cheese
8 fresh basil leaves

Whisk together vinegar, oil, salt and pepper in a bowl. Spray a baking sheet with non-stick vegetable spray. Brush both sides of vegetables with vinegar mixture. Arrange on baking sheet and coat with spray. Broil about 4 inches from heat for 7 minutes, turning once and coating vegetables with spray as needed. Lightly brush one side of each bread slice with remaining vinegar mixture. Place bread, brushed-side down, on an ungreased baking sheet. Top with vegetables, cheese and basil. Top with remaining bread slices, brushed-side up. Place sandwiches in a skillet; set a bacon press or other weight on top. Cook over medium-high heat for about 4 minutes, turning once, until lightly golden on both sides. Makes 4 sandwiches.

*Carol Lytle*
*Columbus, OH*

## fresh from the garden

Keep vegetables fresh longer. Most veggies should be kept in the refrigerator, with the exception of potatoes, sweet potatoes, onions and eggplant. Tomatoes will also keep their sun-ripened flavor best if stored on the counter, not in the refrigerator.

# Herb Garden Sandwiches

8-oz. pkg. cream cheese, softened
½ c. fresh herbs, finely chopped,
    such as parsley, watercress,
    basil, chervil, chives
1 t. lemon juice
⅛ t. hot pepper sauce
8 slices whole-wheat bread,
    crusts removed
paprika to taste

Combine all ingredients except bread and paprika. Spread cream cheese mixture evenly over half of bread slices. Sprinkle with paprika. Top with remaining bread slices; slice diagonally into quarters. Makes 16 sandwiches.

*Lynda Robson*
*Boston, MA*

## tie it up

Asparagus bundles are a great go-with for sandwiches. Steam trimmed asparagus until it's crisp-tender and then transfer to a bowl of ice water to stop the cooking process. Drain; bundle 6 spears together and tie with fresh chive stems. Drizzle with your favorite vinaigrette...so easy!

Penne with Sausage & Cheese

# potluck
## fixin's

In this chapter, you'll find tempting fare sure to please any palate. Wild Rice Hot Dish (page 125) feeds a crowd and will be a requested favorite. For a great make-ahead option, try Potluck Potato Bake (page 136), a cheesy side that comes together in no time with the help of frozen diced potatoes. If you need a dessert for the office party or teachers' luncheon, Cocoa & Coffee Sheet Cake (page 139) is a chocolate lover's dream. And to avoid last-minute panic if you're the hostess, have extra serving dishes and utensils on hand. You'll be glad you did!

# Chicken-Cashew Casserole

For a crispy, crunchy casserole topping, leave the casserole dish uncovered while it's baking. Cover it only if you prefer a softer consistency.

2 10¾-oz. cans cream of
   mushroom soup
⅔ c. water
2 c. cooked chicken, diced
1 c. celery, diced
½ c. onion, grated
6-oz. container cashews

6-oz. can sliced water
   chestnuts, drained and
   coarsely chopped
4-oz. jar sliced mushrooms,
   drained
2 5-oz. cans chow mein noodles,
   divided

In a bowl, combine all ingredients, reserving one can noodles. Spread in a lightly greased 13"x9" baking pan. Bake, uncovered, at 350 degrees for 30 minutes. Sprinkle with remaining noodles; bake for an additional 10 minutes. Serves 6.

*Doris Wilson*
*Denver, IA*

# Cheesy Chicken Enchiladas

2 10¾-oz. cans cream of chicken
   soup
16-oz. container sour cream
4-oz. can diced green chiles
2¼-oz. can chopped black
   olives, drained
3 green onions, chopped

1 onion, chopped
3 c. shredded Cheddar cheese
4 to 5 chicken breasts, cooked
   and diced
10 to 12 10-inch flour tortillas
2 c. shredded Monterey Jack
   cheese

*Toss hot cooked rice with salsa and Mexican cheese blend for a quick & easy side.*

Mix together soup and next 6 ingredients in a large bowl. Set aside 1½ cups of soup mixture for topping; add chicken to remaining mixture. Spoon chicken mixture into tortillas; roll up and place in a lightly greased 13"x9" baking pan. Spoon reserved soup mixture over tortillas; sprinkle with Monterey Jack cheese. Bake, covered, at 350 degrees for one hour. Serves 10 to 12.

*Carrie Kiiskila*
*Racine, WI*

## the more the merrier

Mom's best recipes usually make lots of servings, perfect for sharing. Invite to dinner a neighbor or a co-worker you'd like to get to know better…encourage your kids to invite a friend. You're sure to have a great time together!

# Chicken Spaghetti Deluxe

*This recipe is reminiscent of cold winter days and the inviting smells of Mom's warm kitchen. Best of all, the pasta doesn't need to be cooked ahead of time.*

2 c. cooked chicken, chopped
8-oz. pkg. spaghetti, uncooked
    and broken into 2-inch pieces
1 c. celery, chopped
1 c. onion, chopped
1 c. yellow pepper, chopped

1 c. red pepper, chopped
2 10¾-oz. cans cream of
    mushroom soup
1 c. chicken broth
¼ t. Cajun seasoning or pepper
1 c. shredded Cheddar cheese

Mix chicken, spaghetti, celery, onion, yellow pepper and red pepper in a bowl. Whisk together soup, broth and seasoning in a separate bowl. Add chicken mixture to soup mixture. Spread chicken mixture in a lightly greased 13"x9" baking pan; sprinkle cheese over top. Cover with aluminum foil coated with non-stick vegetable spray. Bake at 350 degrees for 45 minutes. Uncover and bake for 10 more minutes. Serves 8.

*Dorothy Benson*
*Baton Rouge, LA*

Renae's Taco Bake

# Renae's Taco Bake

1 lb. ground beef
1¼-oz. pkg. taco seasoning mix
15-oz. can tomato sauce
3 c. elbow macaroni, cooked
8-oz. container sour cream
1 c. shredded Cheddar cheese, divided
¼ c. grated Parmesan cheese
Garnish: green onions, chopped

Brown beef in a skillet over medium heat; drain. Stir in seasoning mix and tomato sauce. Bring to a boil and remove from heat. Combine cooked macaroni, sour cream and ½ cup Cheddar cheese in a bowl. Spoon macaroni mixture into a lightly greased 13"x9" baking pan. Top with beef mixture and remaining cheeses. Bake, uncovered, at 350 degrees for 30 minutes, or until hot and bubbly. Garnish with green onions. Serves 6.

*Renae Scheiderer*
*Beallsville, OH*

# Chicken Parmigiana Casserole

1 c. Italian-flavored dry bread crumbs
⅓ c. grated Parmesan cheese
1 lb. boneless, skinless chicken breasts, cut into bite-size pieces
2 T. olive oil
16-oz. pkg. penne pasta, cooked
26-oz. jar marinara sauce, divided
1 c. shredded mozzarella cheese, divided

*This is an easy way to get all the flavor of chicken parmigiana without all the fuss!*

Combine bread crumbs and Parmesan cheese in a large heavy-duty plastic zipping bag. Place chicken in bag and shake to coat. Remove chicken from bag; cook in oil in a medium skillet over medium heat until browned on all sides. Layer pasta, half of sauce, half of cheese and chicken in an ungreased 13"x9" baking pan. Top with remaining sauce and cheese. Bake, covered, at 350 degrees for 30 minutes, or until heated through and cheese is melted and bubbly. Serves 6.

# Cornbread-Topped Barbecue Beef

*This recipe sneaks in some veggies for picky eaters!*

2 lbs. ground beef
1 onion, diced
1 green pepper, diced
11-oz. can corn, drained

14½-oz. can diced tomatoes, drained
½ c. barbecue sauce
3 8½-oz. pkgs. cornbread mix

Brown beef and onion in a skillet over medium heat; drain. Add green pepper, corn and tomatoes; cook, stirring occasionally, until vegetables are tender. Stir in sauce; spread mixture in an ungreased 13"x9" baking pan. Prepare cornbread according to package directions; spread batter over beef mixture. Bake, uncovered, at 400 degrees for 20 to 25 minutes, until golden and a knife tip inserted in center comes out clean. Serves 8 to 10.

*Megan Brooks*
*Antioch, TN*

## plan ahead

When chopping onions or celery, it takes only a moment to chop a little extra. Place the veggies in a plastic zipping bag and tuck them away in the freezer for a quick start to dinner another day.

# Beefy Chow Mein Noodle Casserole

2 lbs. ground beef
1 onion, chopped
10¾-oz. can cream of celery
    soup
10¾-oz. can golden mushroom
    soup

1¼ c. water
1 c. instant rice, uncooked
1 T. Worcestershire sauce
1 t. garlic powder
½ t. salt
5-oz. can chow mein noodles

Brown ground beef and onion in a large skillet over medium heat; drain. Stir together soups and remaining ingredients except noodles in a large bowl. Add to beef mixture; mix well. Pour into a lightly greased 13"x9" baking pan. Bake, uncovered, at 375 degrees for 20 minutes, or until bubbly. Sprinkle with chow mein noodles. Bake, uncovered, for an additional 5 to 10 minutes. Serves 16.

*Vicki Cox*
*Bland, MO*

# Florence's Meatball Surprise

1 lb. lean ground beef
1 egg, beaten
1 onion, diced
½ green pepper, diced
salt and pepper to taste
2 10¾-oz. cans cream of
    mushroom soup

1¼ c. water
16-oz. container sour cream
7-oz. pkg. elbow macaroni,
    cooked
15¼-oz. can peas, drained

Mix beef, egg, onion and green pepper in a medium bowl. Add salt and pepper. Shape mixture into small meatballs. Place meatballs in a skillet over medium heat; brown on all sides. Remove from skillet; drain. Blend together soup, water, sour cream and macaroni in a large bowl. Gently stir in meatballs and peas. Pour meatball mixture into a lightly greased 2-quart casserole dish. Bake, covered, at 350 degrees for 30 to 40 minutes. Serves 6 to 8.

*Kim Watkins*
*Wagoner, OK*

## go green

A crisp green salad goes well with almost any comforting main dish. For a zippy lemon dressing, shake up ½ cup olive oil, ⅓ cup fresh lemon juice and a tablespoon of Dijon mustard in a small jar and chill; stir to blend before serving.

Wild Rice Hot Dish

# Wild Rice Hot Dish

2 lbs. ground beef
½ c. butter
1 lb. sliced mushrooms
1 c. onion, chopped
½ c. celery, chopped
2 c. sour cream

¼ c. soy sauce
2 t. salt
¼ t. pepper
2 c. long-grain and wild rice,
    cooked
½ c. slivered almonds

Garnish this hearty dish with a dollop of sour cream, a sprinkle of slivered almonds or fresh parsley, if desired.

Brown beef in a skillet over medium heat. Remove beef from skillet; drain. Melt butter in skillet; sauté mushrooms, onion and celery for 5 to 10 minutes, until tender. Combine sour cream, soy sauce, salt and pepper in a large bowl. Stir in beef, mushroom mixture, cooked rice and almonds. Toss lightly. Place mixture in a greased 3-quart casserole dish. Bake, uncovered, at 350 degrees for one hour, or until heated through. Stir occasionally, adding a little water if needed. Serves 12 to 16.

*June Sabatinos*
*Billings, MT*

# Potato Puff & Ground Beef Casserole

2 lbs. ground beef
10¾-oz. can cream of mushroom
    soup
10¾-oz. can cream of chicken
    soup

1⅓ c. milk
6 c. frozen potato puffs
1½ c. shredded Cheddar cheese

Brown beef in a skillet over medium heat; drain. Stir in soups and milk; heat through. Pour into an ungreased 13"x9" baking pan. Layer potato puffs evenly over top. Bake, uncovered, at 375 degrees for 25 minutes, or until puffs are golden. Sprinkle with cheese. Bake 5 more minutes, or until cheese is melted. Serves 8.

*Tina George*
*El Dorado, AR*

# One-Dish Reuben Dinner

*An easy version of everyone's favorite hot deli sandwich that's always a hit...yummy and filling!*

16-oz. can sauerkraut
1 lb. deli corned beef, chopped
2 c. shredded Swiss cheese
½ c. mayonnaise
¼ c. Thousand Island salad
   dressing

2 c. tomatoes, sliced
¼ to ½ c. pumpernickel or rye
   soft bread crumbs
2 T. butter, melted

Place undrained sauerkraut in a lightly greased 1½-quart casserole dish. Top with corned beef and cheese. Combine mayonnaise and salad dressing; spread over cheese. Arrange tomatoes on top. Toss together bread crumbs and melted butter; sprinkle over top of casserole. Bake, uncovered, at 350 degrees for 25 to 30 minutes. Let stand 5 minutes before serving. Serves 4 to 6.

*Suzanne Ruminski*
*Johnson City, NY*

# Momma Rita's Quick Skillet

1 lb. ground turkey
¼ onion, diced
garlic powder and pepper to taste
2 14½-oz. cans green beans,
    drained

2 15¼-oz. cans corn, drained
2 15-oz. cans diced potatoes,
    drained
seasoned salt to taste
5 to 10 slices American cheese

Brown turkey and onion in a large skillet over medium heat; drain. Add garlic powder and pepper. Stir in green beans, corn and potatoes; season with seasoned salt. Heat through, stirring occasionally. Top with cheese slices as desired. Simmer over low heat about 10 minutes, or until cheese is melted. Stir to combine. Serves 6.

*Rita Bomberry*
*De Soto, MO*

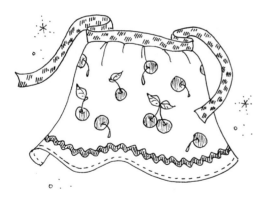

## tie it up

Tie ruffled vintage aprons onto the backs of kitchen chairs for a sweet welcome to a country-style potluck supper.

# Penne with Sausage & Cheese

(pictured on page 112)

1 lb. hot or mild ground Italian
    pork sausage
3 cloves garlic, chopped
24-oz. jar marinara sauce with
    cabernet and herbs
½ t. red pepper flakes
½ t. salt
½ t. pepper
12-oz. pkg. penne pasta, cooked
1 c. shredded mozzarella cheese
Garnish: grated Parmesan
    cheese, chopped fresh
    parsley

Cook sausage in a skillet over medium heat until browned; drain.
Return sausage to pan. Add garlic and cook until tender, about 2 minutes. Stir in sauce and seasonings. Stir sauce mixture into cooked pasta;
pour mixture into a greased 12"x8" baking pan. Top with mozzarella
cheese. Bake, covered, at 375 degrees for 25 to 30 minutes, until bubbly
and cheese has melted. Remove from oven; sprinkle with Parmesan
cheese and parsley. Serves 6.

*Bev Bornheimer*
*Lyons, NY*

# Hearty Pierogie Casserole

2 to 3 16.9-oz. pkgs. frozen
    favorite-flavor pierogies
1½ to 2 lbs. smoked pork
    sausage, sliced into bite-size
    pieces

26-oz. can cream of mushroom
    soup
3¼ c. milk
2 to 3 c. shredded Cheddar
    cheese

Bring a large saucepan of water to a boil; add pierogies and sausage. Cook for 5 to 7 minutes, until pierogies float; drain. Arrange pierogies and sausage in a lightly greased 13"x9" glass baking pan. Blend soup and milk; pour over top of pierogie mixture. Top with cheese. Bake, uncovered, at 350 degrees for 30 to 35 minutes, until soup mixture is bubbly and cheese is lightly golden. Let stand for 5 minutes before serving. Serves 8.

*Sheryl Maksymoski*
*Grand Rapids, MI*

## wrap it up

If you're taking a casserole along to a potluck or carry-in, secure the lid with a brightly colored tea towel wrapped around the baking dish and knotted at the top. Keep the serving spoon handy by tucking it through the knot.

# Party Ham Casserole

8-oz. pkg. medium egg noodles,
    uncooked and divided
10¾-oz. can cream of
    mushroom soup
½ c. milk
1 c. sour cream

2 t. mustard
1 t. dried, minced onion
2 c. cooked ham, cubed
¼ c. dry bread crumbs
1½ T. butter, melted
1 T. grated Parmesan cheese

Measure out half the noodles, reserving the rest for another recipe.
Cook noodles according to package directions; drain. Combine soup
and milk in a small saucepan, stirring over low heat until smooth. Add
sour cream, mustard and onion, stirring to combine well. In a lightly
greased 1½-quart casserole dish, layer half each of cooked noodles,
ham and soup mixture; repeat layers. Toss bread crumbs with melted
butter; sprinkle over casserole. Top with cheese. Bake, uncovered, at
350 degrees for 25 to 30 minutes, until golden. Serves 6.

*Barbara Reese*
*Catawissa, PA*

## cook & share

Potluck dinners are a wonderful way to share fellowship
with family and friends. Why not make a standing date
once a month to try new recipes as well as tried & true
favorites?

# Italian Zucchini Casserole

*Roasted vegetables are delicious and so easy. Drizzle sliced veggies with olive oil, garlic, onion powder, salt and pepper to taste. Arrange on a baking sheet and roast at 350 degrees until crisp-tender.*

3 zucchini, sliced
3 T. olive oil, divided
1 onion, sliced
1 clove garlic, minced
28-oz. can diced tomatoes
1 T. fresh basil, minced

1½ t. fresh oregano, minced
½ t. garlic salt
¼ t. pepper
1½ c. favorite-flavor stuffing mix
½ c. grated Parmesan cheese
¾ c. shredded mozzarella cheese

Cook zucchini in one tablespoon oil in a skillet over medium heat for 5 to 6 minutes, until tender. Drain and remove from skillet. Sauté onion and garlic in remaining oil for one minute. Add tomatoes, basil, oregano, salt and pepper; simmer, uncovered, for 10 minutes. Remove from heat; gently stir in zucchini. Place in an ungreased 13"x9" baking dish. Top with stuffing mix; sprinkle with Parmesan cheese. Cover and bake at 350 degrees for 20 minutes. Uncover and sprinkle with mozzarella cheese. Return to oven and bake for 10 additional minutes, or until cheese is bubbly and golden. Serves 6 to 8.

# Tuna Noodle Supreme

3 T. butter
¼ c. all-purpose flour
2 c. milk
8-oz. pkg. pasteurized process cheese spread, cubed
3 eggs, hard-boiled, peeled and diced

8-oz. pkg. wide egg noodles, cooked
6.4-oz. pkg. tuna, drained and flaked
½ c. sliced mushrooms
salt and pepper to taste
1 c. potato chips, crushed

Melt butter in a large saucepan over medium heat. Stir in flour; cook one minute. Gradually add milk; cook and stir until slightly thickened. Add cheese; stir until melted. Stir in remaining ingredients except chips; mix well. Spoon tuna mixture into a lightly greased 3-quart casserole dish; top with chips. Bake, uncovered, at 350 degrees for 30 minutes, or until hot and bubbly. Serves 6.

Italian Zucchini Casserole

# Potluck Potato Bake

32-oz. pkg. frozen diced potatoes,
    thawed
16-oz. container sour cream
1 onion, chopped
8-oz. pkg. shredded Cheddar
    cheese

10¾-oz. can cream of celery
    soup
¾ c. butter, melted and divided
2 c. corn flake cereal, crushed

Stir together potatoes, sour cream, onion, cheese, soup and ¼ cup butter in a large bowl. Pour into a lightly greased 13"x9" baking pan. Toss together cereal and remaining butter in a medium bowl; spread over potato mixture. Bake, covered, at 350 degrees for one hour and 15 minutes. Uncover and bake for an additional 15 minutes. Serves 16 to 20.

*Trisha Donley*
*Pinedale, WY*

# Texas Corn & Green Chile Casserole

8-oz. pkg. cream cheese
¼ c. butter
¼ c. sugar

16-oz. pkg. frozen corn, thawed
7-oz. can diced green chiles
salt and pepper to taste

Combine cream cheese, butter and sugar in a medium saucepan over medium heat; cook until melted. Add corn and chiles; stir until well blended. Sprinkle with salt and pepper. Pour into a greased 1½-quart casserole dish. Bake, uncovered, at 350 degrees for 30 to 40 minutes, until golden around edges. Serves 10.

*Terri King*
*Granger, TX*

# Company's Coming Fruit Salad

8-oz. pkg. cream cheese,
    softened
¾ c. sugar
10-oz. pkg. frozen sliced
    strawberries, thawed and
    drained
2 bananas, sliced

10-oz. container frozen whipped
    topping, thawed
8-oz. can crushed pineapple,
    drained
1 c. sweetened flaked coconut
1 c. chopped pecans

In a large bowl, blend together cream cheese and sugar with an electric mixer on medium speed. Fold in remaining ingredients by hand. Spread in a 13"x9" baking pan. Cover and freeze 3 to 4 hours, until firm. Remove from freezer a few minutes before serving time; cut into squares. Serves 12.

*Elizabeth Burkhalter*
*Oshkosh, WI*

## display the love

Family recipes make a memory-filled kitchen wall display. Arrange old recipe cards or clippings in a shadowbox purchased at a crafts store, adding cookie cutters and even mini kitchen utensils. To make it all the more special, place a snapshot of Mom or Grandma preparing her favorite recipe.

# Cocoa & Coffee Sheet Cake

2 c. all-purpose flour
2 c. sugar
1 c. butter
1 c. brewed coffee
¼ c. baking cocoa

2 eggs, beaten
½ c. buttermilk
1 t. baking soda
1 t. cinnamon
1 t. vanilla extract

Combine flour and sugar in a large bowl; set aside. Combine butter, coffee and cocoa in a saucepan; bring to a boil. Slowly stir butter mixture into flour mixture. Batter will resemble fudge. Let cool 3 minutes. Stir in eggs and remaining ingredients, mixing until well blended. Pour batter into a greased and floured 13"x9" baking pan. Bake at 350 degrees for 30 to 35 minutes. Pour Chocolate-Pecan Frosting over cake immediately after removing cake from oven. Allow frosting to set before cutting cake. Serves 24.

## Chocolate-Pecan Frosting:

¼ c. baking cocoa
6 T. milk
½ c. butter

16-oz. pkg. powdered sugar
1 t. vanilla extract
½ c. chopped pecans

Combine cocoa, milk and butter in a saucepan; bring to a boil. Add powdered sugar, vanilla and pecans, stirring well. Use immediately.

*Patricia Ivey*
*Lamar, AR*

Deep South Chicken & Dumplings

# back-to-basics

One thing you can bet on is that good old-fashioned home cooking never goes out of style. The earthy aroma of Mama's Scrumptious Roast Beef (page 153) will bring back fond memories of big Sunday dinners at Grandma's house. Wholesome and delicious, Gram Walker's Smothered Chicken (page 143) feeds the body and soul. What better way to wind down the day and bring a smile to little ones…and big ones too…than with a soothing cup of Warm Spiced Milk (page 172) served with a plate of yummy Chocolate Pinwheels (page 172)? The simple recipes found throughout these pages provide comfort for a busy lifestyle.

# Aunt Annie's Chicken Paprika

2 to 3 c. all-purpose flour
1 t. salt
¼ t. pepper
4 lbs. chicken
oil for frying
3 onions, sliced

1 clove garlic, chopped
6 carrots, peeled and sliced
2 T. Hungarian paprika
2 c. water
3 cubes chicken bouillon
spaetzle or egg noodles, cooked

Mix flour, salt and pepper in a large plastic zipping bag. Add chicken pieces, in batches, and toss to coat. Heat 2 tablespoons oil over medium-high heat in a Dutch oven. Sauté onions until tender; remove from pan. Add additional oil to about ½-inch deep. Remove chicken from bag; brown chicken on both sides, in batches; set aside. Stir in remaining ingredients except noodles. Bring to a boil; return chicken to pan. Simmer for one hour over low heat. Serve with cooked spaetzle or noodles. Serves 4 to 6.

*Sandra Lee Smith*
*Quartz Hill, CA*

# Gram Walker's Smothered Chicken

3 to 4 lbs. chicken
1 c. all-purpose flour
salt and pepper to taste
½ c. butter
2.1-oz. env. chicken noodle
   soup mix

10¾-oz. can cream of mushroom
   soup
12-oz. can evaporated milk
1 t. poultry seasoning
dried parsley to taste

Dredge chicken pieces in flour; sprinkle with salt and pepper. Melt
butter in a large skillet over medium heat. Fry chicken until golden on
both sides; transfer to a lightly greased 13"x9" baking pan. Sprinkle
with soup mix; pour mushroom soup over top. Combine remaining
ingredients in a small saucepan over medium heat; heat through without boiling. Pour over chicken. Bake, uncovered, at 350 degrees for
30 minutes, or until chicken is cooked through. Serves 4.

*Dawn Raskiewicz*
*Alliance, NE*

# Chicken Kiev

1½ c. dry bread crumbs
½ c. shredded Parmesan cheese
1 t. dried basil
1 t. dried oregano
½ t. garlic salt
½ t. salt

⅔ c. butter, melted and divided
1½ lbs. chicken tenders
¼ c. white wine or chicken
    broth
¼ c. green onions, chopped
¼ c. dried parsley

Combine bread crumbs, cheese and seasonings in a large bowl. Reserve ¼ cup butter. Dip chicken in remaining melted butter. Roll chicken in crumb mixture. Arrange chicken in a lightly greased 13"x9" baking pan. Bake, covered, at 375 degrees for 30 to 40 minutes, until chicken is tender. Heat wine or broth, green onions, parsley and reserved butter in a small saucepan over medium heat until heated through. Spoon over chicken and bake, covered, for 5 to 7 minutes. Serves 6 to 8.

*Grecia Williams*
*Scottsville, KY*

## buy in bulk

Herbs and spices add lots of flavor to food but can be costly at supermarkets. Instead, purchase them at dollar stores, bulk food stores and even ethnic food stores, where they can be quite a bargain.

# Buttermilk Baked Chicken

¼ c. butter
¼ c. oil
4 chicken breasts
1½ c. buttermilk, divided
1 to 1¼ c. all-purpose flour
1 t. paprika

½ t. garlic powder
½ t. Cajun seasoning
½ t. salt
½ t. pepper
10¾-oz. can cream of mushroom
soup

Melt butter with oil in a 13"x9" baking pan in a 425-degree oven. Dip chicken in ½ cup buttermilk; discard buttermilk. Combine flour and seasonings; dredge chicken. Arrange chicken skin-side down in baking pan. Bake, uncovered, at 425 degrees for 25 minutes. Turn chicken over and bake for 10 more minutes, or until juices run clear when chicken is pierced with a fork. Stir together soup and remaining one cup buttermilk; spoon over chicken. Cover; return to oven for an additional 10 minutes. Serve chicken drizzled with mixture in pan. Serves 4.

*Linda Foreman*
*Locust Grove, OK*

# Deep South Chicken & Dumplings

(pictured on page 140)

3 to 4-lb. roasting chicken
salt and pepper to taste

Garnish: fresh parsley

One of those comfort foods that everybody loves! It's extra special made with homemade broth, but if you're short on time, a good canned broth is fine.

Roast chicken, covered, in an ungreased roasting pan at 350 degrees for 1½ hours. Let chicken cool while preparing Supreme Sauce. Shred chicken; add to simmering sauce. Drop Dumplings into sauce by heaping tablespoonfuls. Cover and cook over high heat 10 to 15 minutes, until dumplings are firm and puffy. Discard bay leaves. Add salt and pepper; garnish with fresh parsley. Serves 6.

## Supreme Sauce:

2 T. butter
1 T. oil
½ c. carrot, peeled and diced
½ c. celery, diced
3 cloves garlic, minced

2 bay leaves
5 T. all-purpose flour
6 c. chicken broth
¼ c. whipping cream

Melt butter and oil in a Dutch oven over medium heat. Add vegetables, garlic and bay leaves. Sauté until soft. Stir in flour; add broth, one cup at a time, stirring well after each addition. Simmer until thickened; stir in cream.

## Dumplings:

2 c. all-purpose flour
1 T. baking powder
1 t. salt

2 eggs
¾ to 1 c. buttermilk, divided

Mix flour, baking powder and salt. Whisk together eggs and ¾ cup buttermilk; fold into flour mixture. Stir just until dough forms, adding a little more buttermilk if needed.

# Mama's Meatloaf

My mother has made this recipe for years. Once you've tried it, you won't want to make any other meatloaf! The glaze is what makes this meatloaf so delicious.

—Maxine

1½ lbs. ground beef
2 eggs, beaten
¾ c. milk
⅔ c. saltine cracker crumbs
salt and pepper to taste

Optional: 2 t. onion, chopped
¼ c. catsup
2 t. brown sugar, packed
1 t. mustard
1 T. lemon juice

Mix together beef, eggs, milk, cracker crumbs, salt, pepper and onion, if desired, in a large bowl. Form into a loaf and place in an ungreased 9"x5" loaf pan. Bake, covered, at 350 degrees for 45 minutes. Mix remaining ingredients; spread over meatloaf. Bake, uncovered, 15 more minutes. Serves 6 to 8.

*Maxine Blakely*
*Seneca, SC*

## a flavorful substitute

Mashed potatoes are the perfect side dish for savory meatloaf. Try a delicious secret the next time you make the potatoes...substitute equal parts chicken broth and whipping cream for the milk...delicious!

# Savory Salisbury Steak

10¾-oz. can golden mushroom
    soup, divided
⅓ c. water
1½ lbs. lean ground beef
1 onion, finely chopped

½ c. dry bread crumbs
1 egg, beaten
½ t. salt
⅛ t. pepper

Mix ¾ cup soup and water in a small bowl; set aside. In a separate bowl, combine remaining soup and remaining ingredients. Form into small patties; arrange in a single layer in a lightly greased 13"x9" baking pan. Bake, uncovered, at 350 degrees for 30 minutes. Drain; spoon reserved soup mixture over patties. Bake, uncovered, 10 to 12 more minutes. Serves 4 to 6.

*Dee Dee Plzak*
*Westmont, IL*

# Granny's Winter Dinner

2 T. oil
1 lb. stew beef, cubed
1 c. water
4-oz. jar button mushrooms,
    undrained
3 potatoes, peeled and sliced

10¾-oz. can cream of mushroom
    soup
¾ c. sour cream
¾ c. milk
1 c. shredded Cheddar cheese

*Add a crisp green salad and a light dessert for a complete meal.*

Heat oil in a large, heavy saucepan over medium heat. Add beef, stirring until browned; drain. Gradually add water and mushrooms. Reduce heat to low; cover and simmer for 2 hours. Transfer beef mixture to an ungreased 13"x9' baking pan; arrange potatoes on top. Combine soup, sour cream and milk in a separate bowl; spoon over potatoes. Sprinkle cheese on top. Bake, uncovered, at 350 degrees for 1½ hours. Serves 4 to 6.

*Martha-Ann Daly*
*Flagstaff, AZ*

## a healthy choice

Use reduced-fat sour cream or cheese in your favorite family recipes. They're just as creamy and good as the full-fat versions and your family won't be able to tell the difference.

# Mama's Scrumptious Roast Beef

14-oz. can garlic-seasoned
    chicken broth
1 c. white wine or chicken broth
3 T. red steak sauce
2 T. brown steak sauce
2 T. balsamic vinegar
2-oz. pkg. onion soup mix
1 T. all-purpose flour

12 to 14 baby carrots
2 red peppers, thinly sliced
2 bunches green onions,
    chopped
5 to 6 cloves garlic, minced
3 to 4-lb. beef rump roast
salt and pepper to taste

I like to strain the excess liquid from the roasting bag and thicken it with flour to make a flavorful gravy.

—Debbie

Combine first 6 ingredients in a large bowl; set aside. Place flour in a large plastic roasting bag; shake bag to coat and arrange in a roasting pan. Place vegetables and garlic in bag; place roast in bag on top of vegetables. Drizzle broth mixture over roast; season with salt and pepper. Cut 6, one-inch holes in top of roasting bag with a knife tip. Seal bag. Bake at 325 degrees for 3 hours, or until roast is tender. Remove roast to a serving platter; let stand 15 minutes before slicing. Serve vegetables with roast. Serves 6 to 8.

*Debbie Donaldson*
*Andalusia, AL*

## try this!

For dark, rich-looking gravy, add a spoonful or 2 of brewed coffee. It will add color to pale gravy but won't affect the flavor.

# Stuffed Green Peppers & Meatballs

6 green peppers
10¾-oz. can tomato soup
1¼ c. water
1 c. instant rice, uncooked
1 lb. ground beef
1 egg, beaten

2 t. onion, grated
2 t. salt
pepper to taste
⅓ c. Italian-flavored dry bread
  crumbs

Slice off tops of peppers; remove seeds and reserve tops. Stir together soup and water; set aside. Combine remaining ingredients in a large bowl; add ⅓ cup soup mixture and mix well. Stuff each pepper with ⅔ cup beef mixture; replace tops. Shape remaining mixture into 2-inch meatballs. Arrange peppers in a lightly greased Dutch oven; add meatballs around peppers. Spoon remaining soup mixture over peppers and meatballs. Bring to a boil. Reduce heat and simmer, covered, for 35 to 45 minutes, basting occasionally. Serves 6.

*Denise Allison*
*Gig Harbor, WA*

## made with love

Food for friends doesn't have to be fancy. Your guests will be delighted with comfort foods like Grandma used to make. Invite them to help themselves from large platters set right on the table...so family-friendly.

# Beefy Cheddar Bake

1 lb. ground beef
1 onion, chopped
1 green pepper, chopped
14½-oz. can diced tomatoes,
    drained
8-oz. pkg. shredded sharp
    Cheddar cheese

2 c. rotini pasta, cooked
10¾-oz. can cream of mushroom
    soup
6-oz. can French fried onions

*What a great dish for sharing! You can even reheat it the next day, and it is still just as good.*

Brown beef, onion and pepper in a skillet over medium-high heat; drain. Combine all ingredients except French fried onions in a large bowl; mix well. Spread into a lightly greased 13"x9" baking pan; cover with aluminum foil. Bake at 350 degrees for 30 minutes. Remove foil; sprinkle with onions. Bake, uncovered, for 5 to 10 minutes. Serves 8 to 12.

*Kimberly Keafer*
*St. Johnsbury, VT*

# Homemade Turkey Pot Pie

*This recipe has been in our family for years...a real treat.*

⅓ c. butter
⅓ c. onion, chopped
⅓ c. all-purpose flour
½ t. salt
¼ t. pepper
1¾ c. turkey broth
⅔ c. milk

2½ to 3 c. cooked turkey, chopped
10-oz. pkg. frozen peas and carrots, thawed
1 14.1-oz pkg. refrigerated pie crusts

Melt butter in a large saucepan over low heat. Stir in onion, flour, salt and pepper. Cook, stirring constantly, until mixture is bubbly; remove from heat. Stir in broth and milk. Heat to boiling, stirring constantly. Boil and stir for one minute. Mix in turkey, peas and carrots; set aside. Roll out one pie crust and place in a 9"x9" baking pan. Pour turkey mixture into pan. Roll remaining crust into an 11-inch square; cut out vents with a small cookie cutter. Place crust over filling; turn edges under and crimp. Bake at 425 degrees for 35 minutes, or until golden. Serves 4 to 6.

*Sarah Sullivan*
*Andrews, NC*

## pick the right size

Choosing a turkey? Allow about one pound per person plus a little extra for leftovers. For example, a 15-pound turkey would serve 12 people with enough left to enjoy turkey sandwiches, turkey tetrazzini or turkey soup afterward.

# Pork Scallopini

2 lbs. pork tenderloin, sliced
　　½-inch thick
1 c. dry bread crumbs
1 c. all-purpose flour
½ t. salt
4 T. butter

4 T. oil
16-oz. pkg. sliced mushrooms
1 c. sherry or chicken broth
1 T. dried parsley
cooked rice or noodles

Place pork slices between 2 sheets of wax paper. Gently flatten to ¼-inch thickness with a rolling pin. Stir together bread crumbs, flour and salt in a large bowl. Coat pork in flour mixture. Cook pork in butter and oil in a large skillet over medium-high heat until golden on both sides and cooked through. Remove pork and keep warm. In same skillet, sauté mushrooms until golden; add sherry or broth and parsley. Stir until all browned bits are dissolved. Serve over rice or noodles. Serves 4 to 6.

*Nan Wysock*
*New Port Richey, FL*

# Grandma Knorberg's Pork Chop Casserole

6 bone-in pork chops
salt and pepper to taste
⅛ t. dried sage
10¾-oz. can cream of mushroom
　　soup

½ c. water
1 c. carrot, peeled and sliced
½ c. celery, sliced

Arrange pork chops in an ungreased 13"x9" baking pan; sprinkle with salt, pepper and sage. Combine remaining ingredients; spoon soup mixture over chops. Bake, covered, at 350 degrees for 45 minutes. Serves 6.

*Shirl Parsons*
*Cape Carteret, NC*

# Pizzeria Sausage Supper

1 lb. ground pork sausage
½ c. onion, chopped
¼ c. green pepper, chopped
2 T. all-purpose flour
16-oz. can diced tomatoes, undrained
4-oz. can mushroom stems & pieces, drained
1 t. fresh oregano, chopped
½ t. fresh basil, chopped
¼ t. garlic powder
⅛ t. pepper
Optional: 4-oz. pkg. sliced pepperoni
10-oz. tube refrigerated biscuits, quartered
2 c. shredded mozzarella cheese
Optional: grated Parmesan cheese

Brown sausage, onion and pepper in a large ovenproof skillet over medium heat. Drain; sprinkle with flour. Add tomatoes, mushrooms, herbs and seasonings; mix well. Simmer until hot and bubbly, stirring until slightly thickened. Add pepperoni, if desired. Arrange biscuit quarters over mixture in skillet. Sprinkle biscuit layer with mozzarella cheese. Bake, uncovered, at 400 degrees for 12 to 16 minutes, until biscuits are golden. Garnish with Parmesan cheese, if desired. Serves 10.

*Kay Jones*
*Cleburne, TX*

My children loved pizza when they were young, like most kids do. When I came across this recipe, I added my own touches, and they loved it because it had all their favorite pizza flavors.

—**Kay**

## best way to freeze

When freezing leftover diced peppers, corn or fresh herbs, add a little olive oil to the plastic zipping bag and shake. The oil will help keep the food separate and fresher too...all ready to drop into sauces and salsas.

# Tuscan Pork Loin

4-lb. boneless pork loin roast
8-oz. pkg. cream cheese, softened
1 T. dried pesto seasoning
½ c. baby spinach
6 slices bacon, crisply cooked
12-oz. jar roasted red peppers,
    drained and divided

1 t. paprika
1 t. salt
½ t. pepper
Garnish: baby spinach

Slice pork lengthwise, cutting down center, but not through other side. Open halves and cut down center of each half, cutting to, but not through other sides. Open pork into a rectangle. Place pork between 2 sheets of heavy-duty plastic wrap and flatten into an even thickness using a rolling pin or the flat side of a meat mallet.

Spread cream cheese evenly over pork. Sprinkle with pesto seasoning; arrange spinach over cream cheese. Top with bacon slices and half of red peppers; reserve remaining red peppers for another recipe. Roll up pork lengthwise; tie at 2-inch intervals with kitchen string. Rub pork with paprika, salt and pepper.

Place roast seam-side down on a lightly greased rack on an aluminum foil-lined baking sheet. Bake at 425 degrees for 30 minutes, or until a meat thermometer inserted into thickest portion registers 145 degrees. Remove from oven; let stand for 10 minutes. Remove string from pork; slice pork into ½-inch thick servings. Serve pork slices on a bed of spinach leaves, if desired. Serves 8 to 10.

*Gina McClenning*
*Valrico, FL*

Guests always ask for this recipe, and leftovers are delicious the next day. Instead of using plain cream cheese, try garlic-and-herb spreadable cheese.

—Gina

# Ham Steak & Apples Skillet

*My grandmother's old black cast-iron skillet brings back wonderful memories of the delicious things she used to make in it. I seek out scrumptious skillet recipes just so I can use Grandma's old skillet...this one is a real family favorite.*

*—Gail*

3 T. butter
½ c. brown sugar, packed
1 T. Dijon mustard

2 c. apples, cored and diced
2 1-lb. bone-in ham steaks

Melt butter in a large skillet over medium heat. Add brown sugar and mustard; bring to a simmer. Add apples; cover and simmer for 5 minutes. Top apples with ham steaks. Cover with a lid; simmer for about 10 more minutes or until apples are tender. Remove ham to a platter and cut into serving-size pieces. Top ham with apples and sauce. Serves 6.

*Gail Prather*
*Hastings, NE*

## country-style centerpiece

The simplest table decorations are often the most charming. Fill a rustic wooden bowl with shiny red apples or fragrant yellow lemons for the kitchen table, or pile the bowl with bright-colored balls of yarn for a crafting corner.

# He-Man Casserole

*This recipe was first published in my church cookbook in 1983. So hearty, filled with ham and mashed potatoes…that must be how it got its name!*

6 T. butter
½ c. onion, chopped
½ c. green pepper, chopped
6 T. all-purpose flour
⅛ t. pepper
1½ c. milk
1 c. chicken broth

4 c. cooked ham, cubed
10-oz. pkg. frozen peas, thawed
    and drained
4 c. mashed potatoes
1 egg, beaten
1 c. shredded Cheddar cheese

Melt butter in a large skillet over medium heat. Add onion and green pepper; cook until tender. Add flour and pepper; stir until smooth. Gradually stir in milk and broth. Cook, stirring until thickened. Stir in ham and peas; pour ham mixture into a lightly greased 3-quart casserole dish. Combine mashed potatoes, egg and cheese in a large bowl. Drop potato mixture by tablespoonfuls onto ham mixture. Bake, uncovered, at 375 degrees for 45 minutes, or until hot and bubbly. Serves 8.

*Linda Barner*
*Fresno, CA*

# Shrimp Creole

2 to 4 T. oil
2 onions, chopped
1 c. celery, chopped
1 green pepper, sliced
8-oz. can tomato sauce
14½-oz. can diced tomatoes
10-oz. can diced tomatoes with
   green chiles
½ c. water
1 bay leaf
2 t. sugar
2 t. Creole seasoning, divided
4 lbs. uncooked large shrimp,
   peeled, deveined and
   cleaned
cooked rice

My grandma used to make this dish whenever we came to visit. I still make it often.

—Robin

Heat oil in a Dutch oven over medium heat. Add onions, celery and green pepper; cook, stirring occasionally, until tender. Add tomato sauce, next 5 ingredients and one teaspoon Creole seasoning; reduce heat to low and simmer for 45 minutes, stirring occasionally. In a separate large stockpot, add shrimp with remaining Creole seasoning and water to cover. Simmer for 5 minutes; drain. Add shrimp to tomato mixture and simmer until heated through. Discard bay leaf before serving. Serve over cooked rice. Serves 8 to 10.

*Robin Glass*
*Hewitt, TX*

# Baked Crumbed Haddock

*Delicious! Serve with mac and cheese and steamed broccoli for a down-home dinner.*

2 5½-oz. pkgs. onion & garlic croutons
1 c. butter, melted

3 lbs. haddock fillets
Optional: lemon slices

Finely grind croutons in a food processor. Toss together croutons and butter. Place fish in a lightly greased 13"x9" baking pan. Sprinkle crouton mixture over fish. Bake, uncovered, at 350 degrees for 20 to 25 minutes, until fish flakes easily with a fork. Top fish with lemon slices, if desired. Serves 6 to 8.

*Michelle Waddington*
*New Bedford, MA*

# Snapper in a Snap

Here on the Gulf Coast we eat a lot of fresh red snapper, so I was happy to find a new way to serve it. This recipe takes just a little of this & that to create a delicious dish.

—Cheri

½ c. lemon juice
¼ c. rice wine vinegar
2 T. olive oil
2 T. honey

2 t. Dijon mustard
1½ t. ground ginger
½ c. green onions, chopped
1 lb. red snapper fillets

Whisk together lemon juice, vinegar, oil, honey, mustard and ginger in a shallow bowl; stir in onions. Heat a non-stick skillet over medium heat. Dip fish fillets in lemon juice mixture to coat both sides; add to skillet. Cook for 2 to 3 minutes on each side. Pour remaining mixture into skillet. Reduce heat to low and simmer for 2 to 3 minutes, until fish flakes easily with a fork. Serves 4.

*Cheri Maxwell*
*Gulf Breeze, FL*

Baked Crumbed Haddock

# 3-Cheese Spinach Rigatoni

*The best part about this dish is that it is on the table in fewer than 30 minutes.*

16-oz. pkg. rigatoni pasta,
    uncooked
3 T. olive oil, divided
10-oz. pkg. frozen chopped
    spinach, thawed and drained
2 c. ricotta cheese
5 T. grated Parmesan cheese,
    divided

¾ t. salt
¼ t. pepper
Optional: ¼ t. nutmeg
1½ c. shredded fontina cheese,
    divided
Garnish: additional grated
    Parmesan cheese

Cook rigatoni according to package directions. Drain; toss with one tablespoon oil and place in a lightly greased 13"x9" baking pan. Combine spinach, ricotta and 3 tablespoons Parmesan in a food processor or blender; purée until smooth. Add salt, pepper and nutmeg, if desired, to spinach mixture. Stir half of fontina into spinach mixture. Pour spinach mixture over rigatoni; top with remaining fontina and Parmesan cheese. Drizzle with remaining oil. Cover and bake at 450 degrees for 15 to 20 minutes, until golden and heated through. Serve with additional Parmesan cheese, if desired. Serves 4.

*Audrey Lett*
*Newark, DE*

## pick a theme

Weekly theme nights make meal planning simple...have family members choose their favorites! They'll look forward to Spaghetti Monday and Tex-Mex Tuesday... you'll always know the answer to "What's for dinner?"

# Mee-Mee's Berry Gelatin

3.4-oz. pkg. raspberry gelatin mix
3.4-oz. pkg. lemon gelatin mix
2 c. boiling water
10-oz. pkg. frozen raspberries,
    thawed
1 c. whole-berry cranberry sauce
8-oz. can crushed pineapple,
    drained

1 c. lemon-lime soda
1 c. milk
¼ c. instant vanilla pudding mix
2 c. frozen whipped topping,
    thawed

Combine gelatin mixes in a medium bowl. Add boiling water; stir well to dissolve. Add raspberries and cranberry sauce to gelatin mixture; mix well. Stir in pineapple. Let cool briefly. Add soda; pour fruit mixture into a 9"x9" serving dish and chill until mixture is set. Whisk together milk and pudding mix for 2 minutes; fold in whipped topping. Spread pudding mixture over gelatin; cut into squares. Serves 6 to 9.

*Brooke Steinke*
*Williams, CA*

## keep it covered & chilled

To maintain its shape, a gelatin-based dessert should be refrigerated until ready to serve. Be sure to store it in a covered container to prevent a thick, rubbery film from forming on the surface.

# Tart Apple Salad

6 tart crisp apples, peeled, cored
    and chopped
1½ c. seedless red grapes, halved
1 c. celery, finely chopped
½ c. chopped walnuts

¼ c. sugar
1 T. mayonnaise-type salad
    dressing
½ pt. whipping cream
¼ c. sweetened dried cranberries

Toss together first 4 ingredients in a large serving bowl; sprinkle with sugar. Stir in salad dressing; mix well. Cover and chill until ready to serve. Beat whipping cream until medium peaks form. Before serving, fold whipped cream and cranberries into fruit mixture. Serve immediately. Serves 10 to 12.

*Leona Krivda*
*Belle Vernon, PA*

# Warm Spiced Milk

*This is a tummy-warming beverage…it's like a baked apple in a mug.*

2½ c. milk
⅓ c. apple butter
2½ T. maple syrup

¼ t. cinnamon
⅛ t. ground cloves

Whisk together all ingredients in a heavy saucepan over low heat until milk steams. Do not boil. Serves 4.

*Loni Ventura*
*Wimauma, FL*

# Chocolate Pinwheels

One night my kids were asking for a quick treat… this was the tasty result!

—Lisa

11-oz. tube refrigerated bread sticks
¾ c. semi-sweet chocolate chips

¼ c. butter, melted
½ c. sugar

Unroll bread sticks and cut them in half. Press chocolate chips in a single row along the top of each bread stick half; roll up into a pinwheel. Arrange pinwheels on a parchment paper-lined baking sheet. Brush with melted butter; sprinkle with sugar. Bake at 350 degrees for 10 to 12 minutes, until golden. Makes 16.

*Lisa Ashton*
*Aston, PA*

Grandmother's Garden
Macaroni Salad

# sensational
# sides & salads

Make any meal complete with one of these appetizing sides &
salads. They're so simple and full of goodness!
Creamy and comforting, Mom's
Macaroni & Cheese (page 177)
delivers a memory in every bite.
Fresh-squeezed lemon juice
gives Lemony Orzo Salad
(page 196) a tangy burst
of flavor and is the perfect

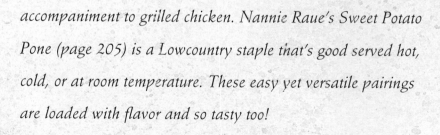

accompaniment to grilled chicken. Nannie Raue's Sweet Potato
Pone (page 205) is a Lowcountry staple that's good served hot,
cold, or at room temperature. These easy yet versatile pairings
are loaded with flavor and so tasty too!

Mom's Macaroni & Cheese

# Mom's Macaroni & Cheese

8-oz. pkg. elbow macaroni,
    uncooked
5-oz. can evaporated milk
1 c. milk
⅓ c. water
3 T. butter

3 T. all-purpose flour
½ t. salt
1 T. dried, minced onion
1½ c. shredded sharp Cheddar
    cheese, divided

Cook macaroni according to package instructions; drain. Combine evaporated milk, milk and water; set aside. Melt butter in a medium saucepan over medium heat. Add flour and salt, whisking until blended. Add onion and evaporated milk mixture, stirring well to avoid lumps. Add one cup cheese. Simmer until cheese melts and sauce is thickened, stirring frequently. Stir in macaroni. Pour into a lightly greased 8"x8" baking pan. Top with remaining cheese and bake, uncovered, at 350 degrees for 30 minutes, or until bubbly and lightly golden. Serves 4 to 6.

*Jenny Newman*
*Goodyear, AZ*

Mom has been making this dish since before I was born. As far as I'm concerned, it's the only way to make mac & cheese! I always think of it as a great comfort food.

—Jenny

# Baked Hominy & Cheese

3 T. butter
¼ c. onion, finely chopped
3 T. all-purpose flour
¾ t. chili powder
salt and pepper to taste

1½ c. milk
2 15-oz. cans white hominy,
    drained and rinsed
1 c. shredded Cheddar cheese

Melt butter in a large saucepan over medium heat; add onion and cook until tender. Add flour and seasonings; cook and stir until bubbly. Slowly add milk; cook and stir until thickened. Stir in hominy; pour mixture into a lightly greased 1½-quart casserole dish. Top with cheese. Bake, uncovered, at 350 degrees for 35 to 40 minutes. Serves 6.

# Herbed Mashed Potatoes

*Filled with fresh herbs, these potatoes are just wonderful! Serve topped with a large pat of melting butter, of course.*

6½ c. potatoes, peeled and cubed
2 cloves garlic, halved
½ c. milk
½ c. sour cream
1 T. butter, softened

2 T. fresh oregano, minced
1 T. fresh parsley, minced
1 T. fresh thyme, minced
¾ t. salt
⅛ t. pepper

Place potatoes and garlic in a large saucepan; cover potatoes with water. Bring to a boil over medium-high heat. Reduce heat to medium; simmer for 20 minutes, or until potatoes are very tender. Drain; return potatoes and garlic to pan. Add remaining ingredients; beat with an electric mixer at medium speed to desired consistency. Serves 6 to 8.

*Vickie*
*Gooseberry Patch*

## keep on hand

Make herbed butter to dress up mashed potatoes or to serve with warm rolls. Simply roll a stick of softened butter in freshly chopped herbs and wrap in plastic wrap. Chill until firm. Better yet, make several variations, label and freeze.

# Sweet & Nutty Couscous

2 c. vegetable broth
5 T. butter, sliced
½ c. dates, chopped
½ c. dried apricots, chopped

½ c. golden raisins
2 c. couscous, uncooked
½ c. slivered almonds, toasted
1 T. cinnamon

Pour broth into a large saucepan; bring to a boil over medium-high heat. Add butter, dates, apricots and raisins; boil for 2 to 3 minutes. Remove from heat; stir in couscous. Cover and let stand 5 minutes. Stir in almonds and cinnamon. Serves 4 to 6.

*Amy Bell*
*Arlington, TN*

## nice & toasty

Toasting really brings out the flavor of shelled nuts. Place nuts in a small dry skillet. Cook and stir over low heat for a few minutes until toasty and golden!

# Red Rice

*Simply delicious with baked chicken or pork chops.*

16-oz. can crushed tomatoes
1 c. long-cooking rice, uncooked
½ c. water
2 T. tomato paste
1½ t. salt
1 t. pepper

6 slices bacon, crisply cooked,
    crumbled and drippings
    reserved
1 c. onion, diced
½ c. green pepper, diced

Combine tomatoes, rice, water, tomato paste, salt and pepper in a medium saucepan; set aside. Heat reserved drippings in a large skillet over medium heat. Add onion and green pepper; cook for one minute. Stir vegetables into tomato mixture; cover. Bring to a boil; reduce heat and simmer for 30 to 35 minutes, until rice is tender. Stir in crumbled bacon. Serves 6.

*Naomi Cooper*
*Delaware, OH*

# Country-Style Pepper Cabbage

*My mother used to fix this simple side for my grandfather...it's still a family favorite!*

4 c. cabbage, thinly sliced
¼ c. onion, chopped
1 c. milk
3 T. butter

1 t. sugar
½ t. salt
½ t. pepper

Combine all ingredients in a 2-quart stockpot over medium heat. Cover and boil for 5 to 10 minutes; do not overcook. Serve piping hot. Serves 4.

*Tonya Adams*
*Magnolia, KY*

# Old-Fashioned Creamed Corn

6 ears corn, husked
¼ c. bacon drippings
¼ c. water
2 T. all-purpose flour

½ c. milk
sugar to taste
salt and pepper to taste

Remove kernels from corn cobs, reserving as much liquid as possible. Set aside. Heat drippings in a cast-iron skillet over medium heat. Add corn and reserved liquid. Stir in water and cook for 15 minutes. Whisk flour into milk; slowly add to corn. Reduce heat to low and cook, stirring frequently, until mixture thickens. Sprinkle with sugar, salt and pepper; stir to blend. Serves 6.

*Beverly Tanner*
*Crouse, NC*

# Fried Green Tomatoes

*Summer squash or okra can also be prepared using this same batter.*

1 c. all-purpose flour
1 c. cornmeal
½ t. salt

½ t. pepper
3 green tomatoes, sliced
oil for frying

Whisk together dry ingredients. Dip tomatoes into mixture. Pour oil to a depth of 2 inches in a Dutch oven or cast-iron skillet; heat to 350 degrees. Fry tomatoes until golden and crispy on both sides. Serves 4.

*Ginny Schneider*
*Muenster, TX*

# Zesty Horseradish Carrots

*This is such an easy make-ahead dish. Assemble it the night before and refrigerate; sprinkle on the topping and then pop it in the oven just before mealtime.*

6 to 8 carrots, peeled and cut
    into matchsticks
½ c. mayonnaise
2 T. onion, grated

2 T. horseradish sauce
½ t. salt
¼ t. pepper

    Cover carrots with water in a saucepan; cook for 6 to 8 minutes over medium heat. Drain, reserving ¼ cup cooking liquid. Combine carrots, reserved cooking liquid and remaining ingredients. Spoon mixture into a lightly greased 9"x9" baking pan; sprinkle with Topping. Bake, uncovered, at 375 degrees for 15 to 20 minutes. Serves 6.

## Topping:

¼ c. bread crumbs
1 T. butter, softened

⅛ t. paprika

    Combine all ingredients; mix until crumbly.

*Joan White*
*Malvern, PA*

# Asparagus with Pecans

1 bunch asparagus, trimmed
1 t. butter

½ c. chopped pecans

*A favorite dish to serve with fish or chicken.*

Place asparagus in a microwave-safe dish. Microwave, covered, on high for 2 minutes. Melt butter in a large saucepan over medium heat. Stir in pecans, stirring constantly, until toasted. Transfer asparagus to saucepan and sauté for 5 to 7 minutes, until tender. Top with pecan mixture. Serves 4.

*Mary Mayall*
*Dracut, MA*

# Spicy Braised Greens

2 T. peanut oil
2 T. garlic, minced
1 T. fresh ginger, peeled and
    grated

½ t. red pepper flakes
1 lb. bok choy, coarsely chopped
¼ c. water
soy sauce to taste

*Napa or savoy cabbage works just as well in this quick and tasty dish.*

Heat oil in a large skillet over medium heat. Add garlic, ginger and red pepper flakes; cook and stir until just beginning to turn golden. Add cabbage; stir to coat. Add water and soy sauce; cover skillet and cook for 3 to 4 minutes, until cabbage is tender. Serves 4 to 6.

*Jill Burton*
*Gooseberry Patch*

## a fresh & healthy alternative

Cutting back on salt? Drizzle steamed vegetables with freshly squeezed lemon juice...you'll never miss the salt.

# Grilled Market Veggies

*I just love to take my roomy market basket to the farmers' market. It's great fun to bring home a bushel of veggies, herbs and new recipes to try!*

2 to 3 zucchini, sliced ¾-inch thick
2 to 3 yellow squash, sliced ¾-inch thick
1 to 2 baby eggplant, sliced ¾-inch thick
1 sweet onion, sliced ¾-inch thick
2 tomatoes, sliced 1-inch thick

½ c. balsamic vinegar
1½ c. olive oil
2 cloves garlic, minced
1 T. sugar
1 T. fresh rosemary, chopped
1 T. fresh oregano, chopped
1 T. fresh basil, chopped
1 T. fresh parsley, chopped
salt and pepper to taste

Combine vegetables in a large bowl. Whisk together remaining ingredients and pour over vegetables. Toss to coat. Marinate for 30 minutes to one hour. Remove vegetables from marinade with a slotted spoon. Arrange on a grill over medium heat. Grill 2 to 5 minutes on each side, basting often with marinade, until tender. Serves 4 to 6.

*Regina Wickline*
*Pebble Beach, CA*

## toasty goodness

Adding toasted garlic and nuts to a favorite side dish can't be beat. Combine chopped nuts with sliced garlic cloves; add to a heavy pan over medium heat. Drizzle with olive oil and toast until golden.

# Caramelized Brussels Sprouts

4 lbs. Brussels sprouts, trimmed
½ c. butter
4 onions, cut into strips
¼ c. red wine vinegar, divided

2 T. sugar
salt and pepper to taste
Optional: ½ c. pistachio nuts,
    chopped

Steam Brussels sprouts for 8 to 10 minutes, until crisp-tender. Melt butter in a deep skillet over medium heat. Add onions and 3 tablespoons vinegar; cook until golden. Add Brussels sprouts, sugar and remaining vinegar. Sauté over medium heat until sprouts are lightly caramelized. Sprinkle with salt and pepper. Sprinkle with nuts, if desired. Serves 8.

*Beth Schlieper*
*Lakewood, CO*

## over the door

Watch for vintage plates at yard sales or flea markets... hang them over a door or group them together on a wall for a simple decorating idea.

# Pecan-Butternut Squash Bake

⅓ c. butter, softened
¾ c. sugar
2 eggs
5-oz. can evaporated milk

¼ t. cinnamon
1 t. vanilla extract
2 c. butternut squash, cooked
    and mashed

In a large bowl, beat together butter and sugar with an electric mixer at medium speed. Beat in eggs, milk, cinnamon and vanilla. Add squash and mix well. Pour into a lightly greased 11"x 8" baking pan. Bake, uncovered, at 350 degrees for 45 minutes, or until set. Sprinkle with Crunchy Topping and bake for 5 to 10 more minutes. May be served hot or cold. Serves 4 to 6.

## Crunchy Topping:

½ c. crispy rice cereal
¼ c. sugar

¼ c. chopped pecans
2 T. butter, melted

Combine all ingredients; mix well.

*Lisa Cameron*
*Twin Falls, ID*

# Confetti Coleslaw

*For an extra-special garnish, cut slits lengthwise in green onions and arrange on top of the coleslaw...mandarin orange sections placed at the tip of each green onion will resemble a flower.*

3 c. coleslaw mix
¾ c. frozen corn, cooked and drained
¼ c. red pepper, diced
¼ c. green pepper, diced
4 T. green onions, chopped and divided

11-oz. can mandarin oranges, drained and divided
½ c. mayonnaise
2 T. sugar
1 T. raspberry vinegar
1 T. lime or lemon juice

Combine coleslaw mix, corn, red pepper, green pepper, 3 tablespoons green onions and oranges, reserving 6 orange sections for garnish. Mix together mayonnaise, sugar, vinegar and juice; blend well. Pour over salad and toss to coat well. Transfer to serving dish. Garnish with reserved orange. Serves 8.

*Dale Evans*
*Frankfort, MI*


# Garlic Vinaigrette

*Add more garlic if you want the flavor to really stand out.*

⅓ c. olive oil
⅓ c. white wine vinegar
2 cloves garlic, minced

1 T. sugar
½ t. salt
⅛ t. pepper

Combine all ingredients in a jar with a tight-fitting lid. Secure lid; shake vigorously to blend. Will stay fresh in the refrigerator for up to 2 weeks. Makes ⅔ cup.

*Nancy Ramsey*
*Delaware, OH*

Confetti Coleslaw

# Bountiful Garden Salad

6 c. spinach, torn
1 lb. romaine lettuce, torn
1 stalk celery, chopped
1 red onion, chopped
1 tomato, chopped
½ cucumber, chopped
1 bunch fresh cilantro, chopped
1 clove garlic, finely chopped

½ orange, peeled and sectioned
¾ c. blackberries, raspberries
  and/or blueberries
¼ c. strawberries, hulled and
  sliced
¼ c. chopped walnuts or pecans,
  toasted
Garnish: croutons

Place all ingredients except croutons in a large salad bowl and toss to mix. Drizzle with Raspberry Dressing; garnish with croutons. Serves 6 to 8.

## Raspberry Dressing:

¾ c. to 1 c. raspberries, crushed
¼ c. raspberry vinegar
1 T. sugar

2 T. lemon juice
1 c. olive oil
salt and pepper to taste

Combine raspberries, vinegar, sugar and juice; slowly drizzle in oil, whisking constantly to blend. Add salt and pepper to taste.

*Joanne Fajack*
*Youngstown, OH*

Grandma always served this salad when we came to visit. We loved to watch her putting together this big beautiful bowl of pretty colors and delicious fruits. She grew most of the produce in her garden, and the nuts came from the grocery store where Grandpa helped out.

—Joanne

## a bit of whimsy

Give homemade salad dressings in sweet vintage bottles tied up with a simple herb bouquet.

# Dilly Cucumber Salad

When I moved to Australia, I brought along my Gooseberry Patch books. I absolutely love your books. I've even introduced some of my new Aussie neighbors to them.

—Debra

4 c. cucumbers, peeled and
    thinly sliced
¾ c. sour cream
1 T. oil
1 t. sugar

½ t. garlic salt
½ t. salt
½ t. white vinegar
¼ t. dill weed

Place cucumbers in a serving bowl. Mix next 6 ingredients in a separate bowl; add to cucumbers and toss to coat. Sprinkle dill weed over salad. Cover and refrigerate for at least one hour. Mix lightly before serving. Serves 5 to 6.

*Debra Holme*
*Victoria, Australia*

# Fresh Ranch Salad Dressing

*Making your own salad dressing is easy, and it has such a fresh flavor. We like this dressing spooned over baked potatoes too.*

30-oz. jar mayonnaise
1 c. milk
1 green onion, finely chopped
⅔ c. grated Parmesan cheese

1 T. vinegar
½ t. dill weed
½ t. Worcestershire sauce
¼ t. pepper

Whisk together all ingredients. Pour into a large jar with a tight-fitting lid. Secure lid and store in refrigerator up to 2 weeks. Makes ½ gallon.

*Barbara Voight*
*Pound, WI*

Dilly Cucumber Salad

# Lemony Orzo Salad

16-oz. pkg. orzo pasta, uncooked
3 to 4 c. baby spinach
¼ c. olive oil
½ c. fresh lemon juice
2 T. garlic powder
2 T. onion powder
2 t. fresh parsley, chopped, or
   1 t. dried parsley

1 t. salt
1 t. pepper
2¼-oz. can sliced black olives,
   drained
1 c. grape tomatoes, halved

Cook pasta according to package directions until just tender; drain. Place spinach in a large bowl; add hot pasta and let stand for 2 to 3 minutes to wilt spinach. Combine remaining ingredients except olives and tomatoes. Mix well; add to pasta. Stir in olives and tomatoes. Serve either warm or chilled. Serves 8 to 10.

*Doreen Freiman*
*Lake Hiawatha, NJ*

## a change of pace

Invite family & friends over for a salad supper. Ask everyone to bring along a favorite salad. You provide crispy bread sticks or a loaf of zucchini bread and a pitcher of iced tea...relax and enjoy!

# Ada's Famous Broccoli Salad

1 lb. bacon, crisply cooked and crumbled
4 bunches broccoli, chopped
1 red onion, chopped
8-oz. pkg. shredded Cheddar cheese
1 c. sugar
1 c. mayonnaise
3 T. red wine vinegar

Toss together bacon, broccoli, onion and cheese in a large bowl; set aside. Combine remaining ingredients; mix well. Add to broccoli mixture; toss and chill for 45 minutes before serving. Serves 8 to 10.

*Becky Jackson*
*Parkersburg, WV*

## pass it on

Take time to share family stories and traditions with your kids over the dinner table! A favorite family recipe can be a super conversation starter.

# Grandmother's Garden Macaroni Salad
(pictured on page 174)

8-oz. pkg. elbow macaroni, cooked
2 c. cooked ham, diced
1 c. Cheddar cheese, cubed
15-oz. can peas, drained
1 tomato, diced
½ c. green pepper, diced
¼ c. onion, diced
1 t. salt
¼ t. pepper
¾ to 1 c. zesty Italian salad dressing

Combine all ingredients except salad dressing in a large bowl. Add dressing to taste. Toss and chill for one hour before serving. Serves 6 to 8.

*Sandy Carpenter*
*Washington, WV*

My grandmother used to prepare this recipe when the whole family got together. We didn't live close by, so when we visited, everyone would drop in. This salad brings back great memories whenever I put it on our table.

—Sandy

# Crunchy Green Bean Salad

*Oh, the flavor of this salad…you'll absolutely love it!*

½ c. honey
⅛ t. cayenne pepper
1½ c. pecan halves
3 T. sherry vinegar
2 t. Dijon mustard
¾ t. salt

½ c. walnut oil
2 lbs. green beans, trimmed
¾ c. sweetened dried cranberries
2 heads Belgian endive, trimmed
   and sliced lengthwise
pepper to taste

Stir together honey and cayenne pepper in a saucepan over medium heat until warm. Stir in pecans; pour mixture onto a parchment paper-lined 13"x9" baking pan. Bake, uncovered, at 350 degrees until golden, about 8 to 10 minutes, stirring occasionally. (Watch carefully so pecans don't burn.) Remove from oven and set aside.

Whisk together vinegar, mustard and salt. Slowly drizzle in oil, whisking constantly to blend. Fill a large bowl with ice and water; set aside. Add beans to a stockpot, cover with water and bring to a boil. Cook over medium heat until tender, about 2 minutes. Drain and plunge into ice water. Drain, pat dry and place in a large serving bowl. Toss with vinegar mixture to coat. Add nut mixture and remaining ingredients. Toss gently. Serve immediately. Serves 12.

*Fran Jimenez*
*Granite Bay, CA*

Warm German Potato Salad

# Warm German Potato Salad

10 lbs. redskin potatoes
1 lb. bacon, chopped
½ c. cider vinegar
1¼ c. water
1¼ c. onion, finely chopped
4 T. sugar

2½ t. salt
5 eggs, hard-boiled, peeled,
    sliced, and divided
sugar and salt
Garnish: paprika

Cover potatoes with water in a large stockpot. Boil until soft but not falling apart; drain. Add bacon to stockpot and fry until crisp. Remove bacon, reserving 4 tablespoons drippings in stockpot. Add vinegar, water, onion, sugar and salt. Cook for 5 to 7 minutes over medium heat, stirring occasionally; remove from heat. Meanwhile, peel and slice warm potatoes. Add potatoes to pot along with bacon and 4 sliced eggs; stir until well coated. Add sugar and salt to taste; spoon salad into a large serving bowl. Top with remaining sliced egg and sprinkle with paprika. Let stand before serving; serve warm. Serves 20.

# Louise's Potato Salad

5 lbs. potatoes, peeled, cubed
    and cooked in salted water
4 eggs, hard-boiled, peeled and
    divided
2 stalks celery, chopped
½ red onion, chopped

¼ c. mayonnaise
1 T. sweet pickle relish
½ t. celery salt
½ t. dried parsley
Garnish: paprika, fresh parsley

Keep potatoes warm while preparing other ingredients. Slice one egg and set aside for garnish. Dice remaining eggs; place in a large bowl and add remaining ingredients except garnish. Add warm potatoes to bowl; toss gently to coat. Garnish with sliced egg, paprika and parsley. Refrigerate until serving time. Serves 10.

*Denise Neal*
*Castle Rock, CO*

This recipe was handed down in my husband's family. His Portuguese grandma made this often...it's one of the things they remember best about her cooking.

—Denise

Nannie Raue's Sweet Potato Pone

# Nannie Raue's Sweet Potato Pone

6 c. sweet potatoes, peeled and
    grated
½ c. all-purpose flour
1 t. cinnamon
1 t. nutmeg
1⅓ c. sugar

1 to 1¼ c. evaporated milk,
    divided
1 egg, beaten
6 T. butter, melted
1 t. vanilla extract
Optional: gingersnap cookies

Combine sweet potatoes, flour, cinnamon, nutmeg and sugar in a large bowl. Add one cup evaporated milk; mix well. Stir in egg, blending well. Add butter and vanilla. Pour into a lightly greased 13"x9" baking pan. Bake, uncovered, at 350 degrees for 1½ hours, stirring frequently. Add more milk if dry. Sprinkle with crumbled gingersnap cookies, if desired. Cut into squares; serve hot or cold. Serves 8 to 10.

*Mary Rabon*
*Mobile, AL*

Sprinkle crumbled gingersnap cookies over sweet potato casseroles for a sweet, crunchy topping.

# Laurel's Fruit Salad

1 pineapple, peeled, cored and
    sliced
1 qt. strawberries, hulled and
    sliced
½ c. blueberries
½ c. raspberries
2 c. Red Delicious apples, cored
    and chopped

4 oranges, peeled and sectioned
2 c. orange juice
1 c. sugar
1 t. vanilla extract
¼ t. almond extract
2 bananas, sliced

Combine first 6 ingredients in a large bowl. Combine next 4 ingredients, stirring until sugar dissolves. Pour over fruit mixture, tossing lightly. Chill 2 to 3 hours before serving. Stir in bananas. Serves 12.

*Laurel Perry*
*Loganville, GA*

Anytime I make this for a church social or potluck, I get requests for the recipe. It's so light and refreshing.

—Laurel

# Tamara's Pickled Beets

Grandma knew how to keep fresh beets from staining her hands while cutting them...she rubbed her hands with vegetable oil first!

—Tamara

⅓ c. sugar
⅓ c. red wine vinegar
⅓ c. water
½ t. cinnamon
¼ t. salt

¼ t. ground cloves
5 whole peppercorns
2 c. red or golden beets, peeled, cooked and sliced, or 16-oz. can sliced beets, drained

Combine all ingredients except beets in a saucepan over medium-high heat. Bring to a boil, stirring constantly. Add beets and return to a boil. Reduce heat and simmer, covered, 5 minutes. Let cool and chill in the liquid for 4 hours to overnight. Store in refrigerator up to 2 weeks. Serves 4 to 6.

*Tamara Ahrens*
*Sparta, MI*

# Spiced Peaches

This has been a family favorite for more than 30 years. Our Thanksgiving dinners wouldn't be complete without Spiced Peaches! This recipe needs to be made at least four days ahead.

—Kimberley

4 16-oz. cans sliced peaches in syrup
2 c. sugar
1 c. cider vinegar

4 4-inch cinnamon sticks
2 t. whole allspice
2 t. ground cloves

Combine all ingredients in a large saucepan over medium heat; bring to a boil. Reduce heat and simmer, uncovered, for 30 minutes, or until liquid is slightly thickened. Let cool; pour into a covered container. Refrigerate for at least 4 days prior to serving. Remove from refrigerator approximately one hour before serving. Serves 8.

*Kimberley Bercaw*
*Ewa Beach, HI*

Tamara's Pickled
Beets

Slow-Cooker Sauerkraut
Pork Roast

# slow-cooker *comfort*

If you are a busy cook, then a slow cooker is a welcome best friend. It's such a treat to come home to the smells of an already prepared meal! Enjoy a bowl of Black Bean Taco Soup (page 215) that's a snap to put together with ingredients found in the pantry. The rich, dark broth of French Onion Soup (page 225) benefits from a long, slow simmer. Try Lemon-Poppy Seed Cake (page 230), full of citrus flavor and crunchy poppy seeds...kind of like an upside-down cake that makes its own custard-like topping. From savory to sweet, these recipes are a cinch to assemble...and the results are oh-so good.

# Slow-Cooker Steak Chili

2 lbs. beef round steak, cut into
    1-inch cubes
1½ c. onion, chopped
2 cloves garlic, minced
2 T. oil
1⅓ c. water, divided
16-oz. jar salsa
2 15-oz. cans kidney beans,
    drained and rinsed
15-oz. can tomato sauce
2 14½-oz. cans diced tomatoes

1 c. celery, chopped
1½ T. chili powder
1 t. ground cumin
1 t. dried oregano
½ t. pepper
⅛ c. all-purpose flour
⅛ c. cornmeal
Garnish: shredded Cheddar
    cheese, sour cream, crushed
    tortilla chips

Brown beef, onion and garlic in oil in a large skillet over medium heat; drain. Add beef mixture to a 5-quart slow cooker. Stir in one cup water and remaining ingredients except flour, cornmeal and garnish; mix well. Cover and cook on low setting for 8 hours. Combine flour, cornmeal and remaining water in a small bowl, whisking until smooth. Add mixture to simmering chili right before serving; stir for 2 minutes, until thickened. Garnish as desired. Serves 8.

*Mignonne Gardner*
*Pleasant Grove, UT*

*All summer, I long for cool, crisp autumn nights. The aroma of simmering chili fills my home and makes me giddy in anticipation of Halloween!*

*—Mignonne*

## rinse it away

Just drain and rinse canned beans before using...you'll be washing away any "tinny" taste. The added bonus is that you'll reduce the sodium content as well.

# 6-Bean Casserole

*I remember my mom making this hearty slow-cooker dish for large gatherings when I was a child. It was my favorite then and still is today, especially after a few small additions.*

1 lb. ground beef, browned
    and drained
½ lb. bacon, crisply cooked and
    crumbled
15-oz. can green beans
15-oz. can yellow wax beans
15-oz. can butter beans
15-oz. can Great Northern beans
16-oz. can light red kidney beans

16-oz. can pork & beans
½ c. onion, chopped
½ c. catsup
1 T. brown sugar, packed
1 t. sugar
1 T. dry mustard
1 t. salt
2 t. white vinegar

Lightly grease the top edge of a 5-quart slow cooker. Add beef and bacon to slow cooker; set aside. Drain all beans except pork & beans; place in a large bowl. Add undrained pork & beans to bowl; stir gently and add to beef mixture in slow cooker. Mix together remaining ingredients; add to slow cooker and stir gently. Cover and cook on high setting for 2 to 3 hours. Serves 8 to 10.

*Andrea Royer-James*
*Indiana, PA*

## turn it into supper

Make it a one-pot meal...add some veggies to a favorite slow-cooker recipe. As they generally take longer to cook, potatoes, carrots and onions should be placed in the bottom and along the sides of a slow cooker, with the meat on top.

# Slow-Cooker Beefy Vegetable Stew

1½ lbs. stew beef, cubed
3 potatoes, peeled and cubed
1 c. baby carrots
1 onion, coarsely chopped
1 clove garlic, minced
1 t. dried oregano
pepper to taste
12-oz. bottle beer or
    non-alcoholic beer

2 T. beef soup base
1½ t. browning and seasoning
    sauce
3 T. all-purpose flour
3 T. butter, melted
1 c. frozen corn
1 c. frozen peas

Combine beef and next 6 ingredients in a 5-quart slow cooker; pour beer over top of beef mixture. Add soup base and browning sauce; mix well. Cover and cook on low setting for 7 to 8 hours. About 30 minutes before serving, increase heat to high setting. Blend together flour and melted butter; add to slow cooker. Stir in frozen corn and peas. Cover and cook on high setting for 20 to 30 minutes, stirring occasionally until vegetables are tender. Serves 4.

*Valerie Sovie*
*Ogdensburg, NY*

# Black Bean Taco Soup

*Since everything is just tossed in the slow cooker, this is perfect for busy days. My family loves it...it's been a huge hit at potlucks as well!*

1 lb. ground beef or turkey,
    browned and drained
1 onion, chopped
28-oz. can crushed tomatoes,
    undrained
15-oz. can black beans,
    undrained
15-oz. can chili beans,
    undrained

15-oz. can corn, undrained
1¼-oz. pkg. taco seasoning mix
1-oz. pkg. ranch salad dressing
    mix
Garnish: tortilla chips,
    shredded Cheddar cheese,
    sour cream

Combine all ingredients except garnish in a 5-quart slow cooker. Cover and cook on low setting for 6 hours. Garnish individual portions as desired. Serves 6 to 8.

*Cari Simons*
*Lawrence, KS*

## food, friends & memories

Choose a crisp fall evening to host a bonfire party. Gather friends of all ages...serve soup or chili, hot cider and s'mores, tell ghost stories and sing songs together. You'll make memories that will last a lifetime!

# Joan's Chicken Stuffing Casserole

*Hearty and filling, this chicken dish will be the first to disappear at any potluck.*

2 6-oz. pkgs. chicken-flavored
    stuffing mix
2 10¾-oz. cans cream of chicken
    soup, divided

½ c. milk
3 c. cooked chicken, cubed
8-oz. pkg. shredded Cheddar
    cheese

Prepare stuffing mix according to package directions; place in a lightly greased 5-quart slow cooker. Stir in one can soup. Stir together remaining soup, milk and chicken in a separate bowl. Add to slow cooker. Sprinkle cheese over top. Cover and cook on high setting for 3 hours or on low setting for 4 to 6 hours. Serves 6.

*Joan Brochu*
*Harwich, MA*

# Elizabeth's Slow-Cooker White Chili

*Garnish with crushed white-corn tortilla chips...a clever use for those broken chips that linger at the bottom of the bag!*

1 lb. boneless, skinless chicken breasts, cooked and shredded
4 15.8-oz. cans Great Northern beans, undrained
16-oz. jar salsa
8-oz. pkg. shredded Pepper Jack cheese

2 t. ground cumin
½ c. chicken broth
Optional: 12-oz. can beer or 1½ c. chicken broth

Combine all ingredients except optional beer or broth in a 5-quart slow cooker. Add beer or broth for a thinner consistency, if desired. Cover and cook on low setting for 4 hours, or until heated through. Serves 6 to 8.

*Elizabeth Tipton*
*Knoxville, TN*

## nifty onion tip

Sometimes a recipe will use only half an onion. Rub the cut side of the remaining half with a little vegetable oil and pop it into a plastic zipping bag...it will stay fresh in the refrigerator for weeks.

# County Fair Italian Sausages

19.76-oz. pkg. Italian pork
   sausages
1 green pepper, sliced
1 onion, sliced
26-oz. jar pasta sauce
5 hoagie rolls, split
5 slices provolone cheese

Brown sausages in a non-stick skillet over medium heat; place in a 4-quart slow cooker. Add pepper and onion; cover with pasta sauce. Cover slow cooker and cook on low setting for 4 to 6 hours. Place sausages in rolls; top with sauce mixture and cheese. Makes 5 sandwiches.

*Dale Duncan*
*Waterloo, IA*

Toast buns slightly before adding shredded or sliced meat or sausages...it takes only a minute and makes such a tasty difference.

# Slow-Cooker Sauerkraut Pork Roast
(pictured on page 208)

*Just add mashed potatoes...everyone will beg for seconds!*

3 to 4-lb. pork roast
1 T. oil
salt and pepper to taste
15-oz. can sauerkraut

Brown pork roast on all sides in oil in a skillet over high heat. Sprinkle with salt and pepper. Place roast in a 5-quart slow cooker; top with sauerkraut. Cover and cook on low setting for 6 to 8 hours. Serves 6 to 8.

*Teresa McBee*
*Billings, MT*

# Apple-Spice Country Ribs

2 to 3 lbs. boneless country
    pork ribs
3 baking apples, cored and cut
    into wedges
1 onion, thinly sliced
⅔ c. apple cider

1 t. cinnamon
1 t. allspice
½ t. salt
¼ t. pepper
mashed potatoes or cooked rice

Place all ingredients except potatoes in a 5-quart slow cooker; stir to coat. Cover and cook on low setting for 7 to 9 hours. Juices will thicken as they cool; stir if separated. Serve with mashed potatoes or hot cooked rice. (If bone-in ribs are used, slice into serving-size portions.) Serves 4 to 6.

*Tammi Miller*
*Attleboro, MA*

## try a new side

Instead of rice or noodles, make a barley pilaf. Simply prepare quick-cooking barley with chicken broth seasoned with a little chopped onion and dried parsley. Filling, quick and tasty!

One fall weekend after apple picking, I tossed together this recipe. I was trying to work apples into everything I could think of to use them up, and I used some of the last ones in this slow-cooker recipe. Once it was done, I wished I'd made it first so I could make it again!

—Tammi

# Barbecue Pulled-Pork Fajitas

*We like to spice up these slow-cooker fajitas with shredded Pepper Jack cheese, guacamole and sour cream.*

2½-lb. boneless pork loin roast,
    trimmed
1 onion, thinly sliced
2 c. barbecue sauce
¾ c. chunky salsa
1 T. chili powder
1 t. ground cumin

16-oz. pkg. frozen stir-fry
    peppers and onions
½ t. salt
18 8 to 10-inch flour tortillas,
    warmed
Toppings: sour cream, shredded
    Mexican cheese, guacamole

Place roast in a 5-quart slow cooker; top with onion. Mix sauce, salsa and spices; pour over roast. Cover and cook on low setting for 8 to 10 hours. Remove roast and place on a cutting board; shred roast with 2 forks. Return to slow cooker and mix well; add stir-fry vegetables and salt. Increase heat to high setting; cover and cook for 30 more minutes, or until mixture is hot and vegetables are tender. With a slotted spoon, fill each warmed tortilla with ½ cup pork mixture and desired toppings. Serves 6 to 8.

*Jackie Valvardi*
*Haddon Heights, NJ*

# Down-on-the-Bayou Gumbo

*You can't help but smile with a bowl of gumbo right in front of you! Using a slow cooker means it's ready when you get home.*

3 T. all-purpose flour
3 T. oil
3 c. chicken broth
½ lb. smoked pork sausage,
    sliced
2 c. frozen okra
14½-oz. can diced tomatoes

1 onion, chopped
1 green pepper, chopped
3 cloves garlic, minced
¼ t. cayenne pepper
¾ lb. cooked medium shrimp,
    tails removed
cooked rice

Stir together flour and oil in a saucepan over medium heat. Cook, stirring constantly, for 5 minutes. Reduce heat to low; cook and stir for 10 minutes, until mixture is reddish brown. Pour broth into a 5-quart slow cooker; stir in flour mixture. Add remaining ingredients except shrimp and rice. Cover and cook on low setting for 7 to 9 hours. Add shrimp to slow cooker; mix well. Cover and cook on low setting for 30 minutes. Ladle gumbo over cooked rice in bowls. Serves 6.

*Sue Neely*
*Greenville, IL*

## last is okay

Fresh herbs may lose flavor after hours of slow cooking. Stir them in near the end of the cooking time or check and add a little more seasoning just before serving.

# French Onion Soup

*Start this soup in the slow cooker after breakfast, and it's ready in time for lunch.*

¼ c. butter
3 c. onion, sliced
1 T. sugar
1 t. salt
2 T. all-purpose flour
4 c. low-sodium beef broth

¼ c. dry white wine or beef
   broth
6 slices French bread
½ c. grated Parmesan cheese
½ c. shredded mozzarella cheese

Melt butter in a skillet over medium heat. Add onion; cook for 15 to 20 minutes, until soft. Stir in sugar and salt; continue to cook and stir until golden. Add flour; mix well. Combine onion mixture, broth and wine or broth in a 4-quart slow cooker. Cover and cook on high setting for 3 to 4 hours. Ladle soup into oven-proof bowls. Top with bread slices; sprinkle with cheeses. Broil until cheese is bubbly and melted. Serves 6.

*Robin Hill*
*Rochester, NY*

## slow cook it

Your favorite stovetop soup, stew or chili recipe can be converted for slow cooking...how convenient! If the soup normally simmers for 1½ to 2 hours, just add all the ingredients to the slow cooker and cook it on low for 6 to 8 hours.

Down-Home Split
Pea Soup

# Down-Home Split Pea Soup

*Let this comfort-food favorite simmer in the slow cooker all afternoon.*

8 c. water
2 c. dried split peas, sorted
   and rinsed
1½ c. celery, sliced
1½ c. carrot, peeled and sliced

1 onion, sliced
2 bay leaves
salt and pepper to taste
1 to 2 c. cooked ham, cubed

Combine all ingredients in a 4-quart slow cooker. Cover and cook on low for 4 to 6 hours. Discard bay leaves before serving. Serves 8 to 10.

*Jude Trimnal*
*Brevard, NC*

# Louisiana Red Beans & Rice

2 15-oz. cans red beans,
   undrained
14½-oz. can diced tomatoes,
   undrained
½ c. celery, chopped
½ c. green pepper, chopped

½ c. green onions, chopped
2 cloves garlic, minced
1 to 2 t. hot pepper sauce
1 t. Worcestershire sauce
1 bay leaf
cooked rice

Combine all ingredients except rice in a 4-quart slow cooker. Cover and cook on low setting for 4 to 6 hours. About 30 minutes before serving, use a potato masher to lightly mash some of the mixture until thickened. Cover again; increase heat to high setting and continue cooking for 30 minutes. Discard bay leaf. To serve, ladle over cooked rice in bowls. Serves 6.

*Diana Chaney*
*Olathe, KS*

My mother-in-law, who is from down South, shared this recipe with me. Those Southerners really know how to make something tasty from almost nothing! Sometimes we enjoy this as a meatless meal; other times I'll add a half pound of sliced smoked sausage.

—Diana

# Simmered Autumn Applesauce

*The kids will love this recipe! It's perfect for the apples you picked together at the orchard. Let the delicious aroma from your slow cooker fill your kitchen on a crisp fall day.*

8 apples, several different
    varieties, cored, peeled and
    cubed
1 c. water

½ c. brown sugar, packed
1 t. cinnamon
½ t. pumpkin pie spice

Add all ingredients to a 3 to 4-quart slow cooker; stir. Cover and cook on low setting for 6 to 8 hours. Mash apples with the back of a spoon; stir again. Let cool slightly before serving. Serves 6.

*Jennifer Levy*
*Warners, NY*

## dip for apples

Homemade caramel apple dip...yum! Spray a slow cooker with non-stick vegetable spray and pour in 2 cans of sweetened condensed milk. Cover and cook on low setting for 2½ hours or until milk thickens; stir. Cover and continue cooking another one to 1½ hours, stirring every 15 minutes, until thick and golden. Serve warm or chilled; store tightly covered in the refrigerator.

# Tahitian Rice Pudding

*Scrumptious served warm from the slow cooker or cold.*

¾ c. long-cooking rice, uncooked
15-oz. can cream of coconut
12-oz. can evaporated milk

2¾ c. water
Optional: 1 T. dark rum
⅔ c. sweetened flaked coconut

Stir together rice, cream, milk and water in a 3 to 4-quart slow cooker until combined. Cover and cook on low setting for 4 to 5 hours. Remove crock from slow cooker. Stir in rum, if desired. Let pudding cool for 10 minutes. Heat a small non-stick skillet over medium heat. Add coconut; cook and stir for 4 to 5 minutes, until toasted. Remove coconut and set aside. Spoon pudding into dessert bowls; sprinkle with toasted coconut. Serves 6 to 8.

*Beth Kramer*
*Port Saint Lucie, FL*

# Lemon-Poppy Seed Cake

15.8-oz. lemon-poppy seed
   bread mix
1 egg, beaten
8-oz. container sour cream

1¼ c. water, divided
½ c. sugar
¼ c. lemon juice
1 T. butter

Combine bread mix, egg, sour cream and ½ cup water in a bowl. Stir until well moistened; spread in a lightly greased 3 to 4-quart slow cooker. Combine ¾ cup water and remaining ingredients in a small saucepan; bring to a boil. Pour boiling mixture over batter in slow cooker. Cover and cook on high setting for 2 to 2½ hours, until edges are golden. Turn off slow cooker; let cake cool in slow cooker for 30 minutes with lid ajar. When cool enough to handle, hold a large plate over top of slow cooker and invert to turn out cake. Serves 10 to 12.

*Rogene Rogers*
*Bemidji, MN*

Top-Prize Chicken Casserole

# easy make-ahead
## meals & more

Get a jump start on meal prep or gift-giving from a tasty selection of mains, breads and condiments. Serve the family buttery and tasty Mary's Heavenly Chicken (page 237), soaked overnight in a seasoned marinade. Store-bought broth is handy, but Chicken Broth from Scratch (page 247) imparts wholesome goodness to homemade soups and sauces. Green Tomato Piccalilli (page 251) tastes like summer straight from the jar. You'll find what you're looking for here with dishes to serve and share with the ones you love.

# Grammy's Oatmeal-Buttermilk Pancakes

Whenever we visit Grammy, these yummy pancakes are on the breakfast table without fail...usually surrounded by sausage or bacon, scrambled eggs and toast with jam. We can't imagine breakfast any other way!

—Regina

2 c. long-cooking oats, uncooked
2 c. plus ¼ c. buttermilk, divided
½ c. all-purpose flour
½ c. whole-wheat flour
2 t. sugar
1½ t. baking powder
1½ t. baking soda
1 t. salt
2 eggs
2 T. butter, melted and cooled
butter
warm maple syrup

Combine oats and 2 cups buttermilk in a bowl; cover and refrigerate overnight. To prepare pancakes, sift together flours, sugar, baking powder, baking soda and salt. Set aside. Beat together eggs and butter in a large bowl. Stir egg mixture into oat mixture. Add flour mixture, stirring well. If batter is too thick, stir in 2 to 4 tablespoons remaining buttermilk. Pour batter by heaping tablespoonfuls onto a well-greased hot griddle. Cook until bubbles appear on the surface; flip and continue cooking until golden. Top with butter and maple syrup. Makes 2 dozen.

*Regina Ferrigno*
*Gooseberry Patch*

## a simple substitute

No buttermilk? Stir one tablespoon vinegar or lemon juice into one cup milk and let stand 5 minutes.

# Top-Prize Chicken Casserole

(pictured on page 232)

*This crowd-pleasing dish has graced my family's table for decades. Originally prepared by my mother-in-law, it's been taken to many potlucks and church suppers. With its creamy sauce and crunchy topping, it's always a hit.*

2 to 3 c. cooked chicken, cubed
2 10¾-oz. cans cream of
    mushroom soup
4 eggs, hard-boiled, peeled and
    chopped
1 onion, chopped

1½ c. celery, chopped
2 c. cooked rice
1 c. mayonnaise
2 T. lemon juice
3-oz. pkg. slivered almonds
5-oz. can chow mein noodles

Combine all ingredients except almonds and noodles in a large bowl; mix well. Place chicken mixture in a lightly greased 3-quart casserole dish. Cover and refrigerate 8 hours to overnight. Stir in almonds. Bake, uncovered, at 350 degrees for 40 to 45 minutes, until heated through. Top with noodles; bake 5 more minutes. Serves 6 to 8.

*Betty Lou Wright*
*Hendersonville, TN*

# Mary's Heavenly Chicken

*My stepmom introduced me to this chicken dish when I was about 10 years old. It's a recipe her neighbor gave to her, hence the name. It has since become a favorite of my husband and many of our family members.*

1 c. sour cream
1 T. lemon juice
2 t. Worcestershire sauce
2 cloves garlic, finely chopped
2 t. celery salt
1 t. paprika
½ t. pepper

6 boneless, skinless chicken
   breasts
1½ c. Italian-flavored dry bread
   crumbs
¼ c. butter, melted and divided
cooked rice or noodles

Combine sour cream, juice, Worcestershire sauce, garlic, salt, paprika and pepper in a large bowl. Add chicken and coat well. Cover and refrigerate overnight. Remove chicken from mixture and roll in bread crumbs. Arrange in a single layer in a lightly greased 15"x10" jelly-roll pan. Spoon melted butter over chicken. Bake, uncovered, at 350 degrees for 25 minutes, until juices run clear when chicken is pierced with a fork. Serve over rice or noodles. Serves 4 to 6.

*Julie Otto*
*Fountainville, PA*

## memorable weeknight dinner

Make meals extra special for your family! Even if no guests are coming for dinner, pull out the good china and light some candles...you'll be making memories together.

# Make-Ahead Faux Lasagna

This recipe came from a 1980 North Dakota church cookbook. It is a big hit...as tasty as lasagna but without the effort. That's how the name came about!

—Juanita

16-oz. pkg. wide egg noodles, uncooked
1 T. butter, melted
8-oz. pkg. cream cheese, softened
1 c. cottage cheese with chives
½ c. sour cream
1 lb. ground beef
⅓ c. dried, minced onion
8-oz. can tomato sauce
salt and pepper to taste

Boil half the package of noodles for 5 minutes; drain. Reserve remaining uncooked noodles for another use. Arrange half the cooked noodles in a lightly greased 2-quart casserole dish. Drizzle evenly with melted butter. Combine cheeses and sour cream in a medium bowl. Spoon cream cheese mixture over noodles. Arrange remaining noodles on top; set aside. Brown beef and onion in a skillet over medium heat; drain well. Combine with tomato sauce, salt and pepper; spoon over noodles. Cover and refrigerate for one to 8 hours. Uncover and bake at 350 degrees for 30 minutes. Cover with aluminum foil and bake for 15 more minutes. Serves 10 to 12.

*Juanita Lint*
*Forest Grove, OR*

# Overnight Scalloped Turkey

2 10¾-oz. cans cream of mushroom soup
2½ c. milk
8-oz. pkg. pasteurized process cheese spread, cubed
4 c. cooked turkey, chopped
7-oz. pkg. elbow macaroni, uncooked
3 eggs, hard-boiled, peeled and chopped
½ c. butter, melted and divided
1½ c. soft bread crumbs

Combine soup, milk and cheese in a large bowl; add turkey, macaroni and eggs. Stir in ¼ cup melted butter; transfer to a lightly greased 13"x9" baking pan. Cover and refrigerate for 8 hours or overnight. Toss bread crumbs with remaining butter; sprinkle over top. Bake, uncovered, at 350 degrees for 45 to 50 minutes. Serves 8 to 10.

# Gran-Gran's Sweet Bread

½ c. butter, softened
½ c. shortening
2 c. sugar
3 eggs, beaten
2 t. vanilla extract
2 env. active dry yeast
1 c. warm water

8 c. all-purpose flour
½ t. salt
2 c. warm milk
16-oz. pkg. raisins
½ c. butter, melted
¼ c. sugar

Blend together butter and shortening in a very large bowl. Gradually add sugar, eggs and vanilla, beating well after each addition. Combine yeast and warm water (110 to 115 degrees) in a cup; let stand 5 minutes. Whisk together flour and salt. With a large wooden spoon, gradually stir flour and salt into butter mixture alternately with yeast mixture and warm milk. Mix well; stir in raisins.

Turn dough out onto a floured surface. Knead, adding additional flour until dough is smooth and elastic. Return dough to bowl. Lightly spray dough with non-stick vegetable spray; cover with wax paper and a tea towel. Let rise 6 to 8 hours or overnight, until double in bulk. Punch down; divide into 6 equal portions and place in 6 greased 9"x5" loaf pans. Cover and let rise again until rounded, 4 to 6 hours. Drizzle melted butter over loaves; sprinkle each loaf with 2 teaspoons sugar. Bake at 350 degrees for 30 minutes, or until a toothpick inserted in center comes out clean. Cool on wire racks. Makes 6 loaves.

*Susan Rodgers*
*Mohnton, PA*

As a child, I always looked forward to my grandmother bringing a loaf of her sweet bread every Easter and Christmas. She didn't use a written recipe, so one time I asked her how she made it, and I wrote it down. It took me several tries until I felt it was as good as Gran-Gran's bread. Thank you, Gran!

—Susan

## bread dough tip

Here's how to tell when rising dough has doubled in bulk. Press two fingertips ½-inch deep into the dough and then release. If the dent remains, the dough has doubled.

# Cheesy Batter Bread

4 c. all-purpose flour, divided
2 T. sugar
1½ t. salt
2 env. active dry yeast
1½ c. shredded Cheddar cheese

1 c. milk
1 c. water
2 T. butter
1 egg, beaten

Combine 1⅓ cups flour, sugar, salt, yeast and cheese in a large bowl; set aside. Combine milk, water and butter in a saucepan over medium-low heat until very warm and butter is almost melted (110 to 115 degrees). Gradually stir milk mixture into dry ingredients. Beat at medium speed with an electric mixer for 2 minutes.

Add egg and one cup of remaining flour; increase speed to high and beat for 2 minutes. With a wooden spoon, stir in enough remaining flour to make a stiff batter. Cover dough with a tea towel and let rest for 10 minutes.

Pour into 2 lightly greased 9"x5" loaf pans. Cover and let rise in a warm draft-free place until double in bulk, about one hour. Bake at 375 degrees for 20 to 30 minutes, until lightly golden. Remove loaves from pans; cool on wire racks. Makes 2 loaves.

*Wendy Meadows*
*Gratis, OH*

# Honey-Wheat Bread

*Nothing makes your home smell more inviting than homemade bread baking in the oven!*

½ c. honey
2 env. active dry yeast
2 t. salt
2 c. milk
4½ c. all-purpose flour

4 c. whole-wheat flour
2 eggs, beaten
½ c. butter, melted
Garnish: additional melted
    butter

Mix together honey, yeast and salt in a very large bowl; set aside. Heat milk until warm (110 to 115 degrees). Add milk and next 4 ingredients to honey mixture. Knead until a smooth, stretchy consistency is reached. Place in a greased bowl, cover dough with a tea towel and set in a warm place. Let rise until double in bulk, about 2 to 3 hours. Punch down; divide dough and form into 5 round loaves. Place loaves on lightly greased baking sheets, 2 to 3 loaves per sheet. Let rise for one more hour. Bake at 350 degrees for 25 to 30 minutes. Remove from oven and brush tops of loaves with butter. Makes 5 loaves.

*Brenda Ervin*
*Festus, MO*

## decorative storage containers

Watch for vintage clear glass canisters at flea markets and tag sales. They're handy for storing flour, sugar, pasta and other staples in the kitchen and pantry. You can even color-coordinate the metal lids with a spritz of spray paint.

# Mother's Rolls

1 env. active dry yeast
¾ c. warm water
3½ c. biscuit baking mix,
    divided

1 T. sugar
¼ c. butter, melted
Garnish: additional melted
    butter

Dissolve yeast in warm water (110 to 115 degrees); let stand 5 minutes. Place 2½ cups biscuit mix in a large bowl; stir in sugar. Add yeast mixture, stirring vigorously. Sprinkle work surface generously with remaining biscuit mix. Place dough on surface and knead 15 to 20 times. Shape heaping tablespoons of dough into balls; arrange on a lightly greased baking sheet. Cover dough with a damp tea towel; set aside in a warm place to rise, about one hour. Brush rolls with melted butter. Bake at 400 degrees for 12 to 15 minutes, until golden. Remove rolls from oven; brush again with melted butter while hot. Makes 15 rolls.

*Amy Hansen*
*Louisville, KY*

Growing up, we couldn't wait until Mother's rolls were out of the oven and ready to enjoy. Now that I have a family of my own, my children can hardly wait for them to be cool enough to eat!

—Amy

## microwave magic

A convenient place to let yeast dough rise is inside your microwave. Heat a mug of water on high for 2 minutes. Then remove the mug, place the covered bowl of dough inside and close the door.

# Helen's Homemade Pasta Sauce

Twenty-six pounds of tomatoes may seem like a lot...it's half a bushel basket, so look for those farmers' market specials. This recipe makes a scrumptious sauce for lasagna and stuffed green peppers.

26 lbs. tomatoes, cored, peeled and chopped
3 lbs. onions, chopped
2 hot peppers, chopped
2 green peppers, chopped
8 6-oz. cans tomato paste
1½ c. oil
2 c. sugar
½ c. salt
2 T. dried oregano
2 T. dried basil
2 T. fresh parsley, chopped
½ T. garlic salt or powder
6 bay leaves
11 1-qt. freezer-safe plastic containers and lids, sterilized

Purée tomatoes in a food processor in batches. Place tomatoes, onions and peppers in a very large stockpot. Cook over medium-low heat for one hour, stirring often. Mix in remaining ingredients except containers; continue cooking for 1½ hours, stirring frequently to prevent sticking. Let cool; discard bay leaves. Ladle sauce into freezer containers; secure lids and freeze. Makes 11 containers.

*Linda Fleisher*
*Akron, OH*

## "X" marks the spot!

Peel lots of tomatoes in a jiffy! Cut an "X" in the base of each tomato and place them in a deep saucepan. Carefully add boiling water to cover. After 20 to 30 seconds, remove the tomatoes with a slotted spoon and drop them into a sinkful of ice water. The peels will slip right off.

# Chicken Broth from Scratch

*Everyone needs a good recipe for homemade chicken broth! Use the broth right away in a recipe or freeze for later use.*

3 to 4-lb. roasting chicken
2 carrots, peeled and thickly
    sliced
2 stalks celery, thickly sliced
1 onion, halved
1 clove garlic, halved

2 T. olive oil
2 qts. cold water
4 sprigs fresh parsley
4 sprigs fresh thyme
2 bay leaves
Optional: salt and pepper to taste

Place chicken in an ungreased roasting pan. Cover and roast at 350 degrees for 1½ hours, or until juices run clear when chicken is pierced with a fork. Cool chicken and shred. Reserve pan drippings and bones. Use shredded chicken in your favorite recipe or freeze for later use. Sauté vegetables and garlic in oil in a stockpot over medium heat for 3 minutes. Add reserved bones, pan drippings, water and seasonings; simmer for one hour. Strain broth; season with salt and pepper, if desired. Makes about 8 cups.

*Christian Brown*
*Killeen, TX*

# Buttery Lemon Curd

*A treasured recipe from jolly ol' England! This lemony spread is irresistible on scones, toast and muffins…even on slices of pound cake!*

When recipes require you to zest, it is best to use unwaxed or organic citrus fruits. Besides being free from pesticides, they also deliver the best flavor.

1 c. butter
2 c. sugar
3 eggs, beaten

1 T. lemon zest
½ c. lemon juice

Melt butter in a double boiler over simmering water. Stir in remaining ingredients. Cook, stirring occasionally, for one hour, or until mixture reaches 160 degrees on a candy thermometer. Once thickened, lemon mixture should coat the back of a spoon. Pour into a bowl. Place plastic wrap directly on warm curd to prevent a film from forming. Chill at least 4 hours before serving. Makes 3 cups.

*Sandy Roy*
*Crestwood, KY*

# Easy Pear Honey

Dad was a beekeeper, so Mom was always looking for new ways to use the honey. This recipe's a keeper!

—Cheri

4 c. pears, cored, peeled and
    sliced
1 lemon, thinly sliced
1½ c. sugar
½ c. honey

1 T. water
⅛ t. salt
3 ½-pt. canning jars and lids,
    sterilized
Optional: 3 sprigs fresh rosemary

Combine all ingredients except jars and rosemary in a saucepan over medium heat. Bring to a boil; cook until sugar dissolves. Reduce heat and simmer for 15 minutes, stirring often. Spoon into hot sterilized jars, leaving ¼-inch headspace; add one sprig rosemary, if desired, to each jar. Remove air bubbles; wipe rims. Cover at once with metal lids and screw on bands. Process in a boiling-water bath for 10 minutes; set jars on a towel to cool. Check for seals. Makes 3 jars.

*Cheri Maxwell*
*Gulf Breeze, FL*

Buttery Lemon Curd

Green Tomato Piccalilli

# Green Tomato Piccalilli

8 c. green tomatoes, cored,
 peeled and chopped
2 c. green pepper, chopped
2 c. onion, chopped
3 c. sugar

2 c. white vinegar
¼ c. canning salt
1½-oz. jar pickling spice
7 1-pt. canning jars and lids,
 sterilized

Mix together all ingredients except spice and jars in a stockpot. Place spice in a small cheesecloth bag and add to pot. Simmer over medium heat for 30 minutes, stirring occasionally. Discard spice bag. Spoon mixture into hot sterilized jars, leaving ½-inch headspace. Remove air bubbles; wipe rims. Cover at once with metal lids and screw on bands. Process in a boiling-water bath for 10 minutes. Set jars on a towel to cool; check for seals. Makes about 7 jars.

*Patsy Johnson*
*Salem, MO*

This is one of my mom's recipes, and it is so good! Once I tried this, I couldn't stop eating it. It is an old-fashioned sweet relish and very addictive...really tasty served on the side.

—**Patsy**

# The Best Freezer Pickles

*You can count on this tried & true recipe when the cucumbers really begin to come in during high summer!*

4 c. cucumbers, thinly sliced
Optional: 1 to 2 c. onion, thinly
 sliced
2 T. salt
2 T. water

1 c. sugar
½ c. cider vinegar
1 t. dill weed
4 ½-pt. freezer-safe plastic
 containers and lids, sterilized

Mix cucumbers, onion, if desired, salt and water in a bowl. Let stand for 2 hours; drain. Add remaining ingredients except containers to cucumber mixture. Let stand 2 hours, or until sugar is dissolved and liquid covers vegetables. Spoon into sterilized containers, leaving ½-inch headspace; secure lids and freeze. Thaw in refrigerator before using. Makes 4 containers.

# Fresh Peach Freezer Jam

3 c. peaches, pitted, peeled and
    finely chopped
4½ c. sugar
2 T. lemon juice

¾ c. water
1¾-oz. pkg. powdered pectin
6 ½-pt. freezer-safe plastic
    containers and lids, sterilized

    Combine peaches, sugar and lemon juice in a large bowl; let stand
10 minutes, stirring occasionally. Mix water and pectin in a saucepan.
Bring to a boil over high heat, stirring constantly. Continue boiling
and stirring one minute; add to peach mixture, stirring until sugar is
dissolved. Spoon into sterilized containers, leaving ½-inch headspace;
secure lids. Let stand at room temperature 24 hours. Place in freezer.
Thaw in refrigerator before using. Makes 6 containers.

*Sherry Gordon*
*Arlington Heights, IL*

*I absolutely love the taste
of summertime peaches,
and this jam lets me
enjoy that sweet flavor
even when it's snowing
outside!*

**—Sherry**

## can't wait...enjoy now

If you find freezer jams, jellies or pickles too tempting to
freeze, you can keep them fresh in the refrigerator up
to 3 weeks.

# Italian Bread Crumbs

This is thrifty twice...use up leftover bread and save on store-bought bread crumbs at the same time! Add seasoned bread crumbs directly to a recipe without thawing, or thaw them briefly at room temperature.

—Melody

12 slices bread
1 t. dried parsley
1 t. garlic powder
1 t. onion powder
1 t. sugar
1 t. salt
½ t. pepper
½ t. Italian seasoning

Place bread on a baking sheet and bake at 300 degrees for about 15 minutes, or until dried out. Tear slices into pieces and process to fine crumbs in a food processor. Add remaining ingredients; process until combined. Place in a freezer-safe container; keep frozen. Makes about 4 cups.

*Melody Taynor*
*Everett, WA*

# Annette's Raspberry Vinegar

*The light flavor of this vinegar is perfect drizzled over crisp salads.*

1½ c. white vinegar
½ c. sugar
1 c. raspberries

Combine vinegar and sugar in a saucepan over medium heat. Cook, stirring occasionally, until hot but not boiling. Pour into a glass bowl; stir in raspberries. Cover with plastic wrap and let stand in a cool place 6 to 7 days. Strain through cheesecloth twice; pour into a sterilized jar or bottle with a tight-fitting lid. Store in refrigerator for up to 2 months. Makes 1½ to 2 cups.

*Annette Ingram*
*Grand Rapids, MI*

# Basil Pesto

*Pesto is delicious spread on a sandwich or layered with almost any appetizer dip. Try spreading it over a thin cut of meat or fish; then coat with bread crumbs and place on the grill.*

| | |
|---|---|
| 1 c. fresh basil | ½ t. salt |
| 1 c. baby spinach | ¼ t. pepper |
| ¼ c. pine nuts | ½ c. olive oil |
| ¼ c. grated Romano cheese | ½ c. vegetable oil |
| 2 T. garlic, minced | |

Combine all ingredients except oils in a food processor. Pulse on and off 5 to 6 times to chop basil and spinach. With the motor running, add oils in a slow stream until mixture is creamy in texture. Spoon mixture into ice cube trays and freeze. Pop out and place in plastic freezer bags; freeze until ready to use in your favorite recipe. Makes about 2 cups.

*Kay Barg*
*Sandy, UT*

## spread on the flavor

Fresh basil makes the most delicious basil butter. Measure 1½ cups packed leaves and then finely chop... kitchen scissors are great for this. Add basil to 2 cups softened butter; blend well. Basil butter is extra tasty on grilled foods or steamed veggies.

# Traveling Fudge

*I have been sending goodies to my overseas military family members so that they can have a taste of home. It arrives fine, and everyone loves it. I thought I'd share the recipe for Traveling Fudge so that others can send some to their families.*

3 c. sugar
1 c. evaporated milk
½ c. butter
12-oz. pkg. semi-sweet chocolate
   chips

1 c. marshmallow creme
1 t. vanilla extract
Optional: 1 c. coarsely chopped
   pecans or walnuts

Bring sugar, milk and butter to a rolling boil in a heavy 5-quart Dutch oven over medium heat, stirring until sugar dissolves. Cook, stirring constantly to prevent scorching, to the soft-ball stage, or 234 to 243 degrees on a candy thermometer. Remove from heat. Stir in chocolate chips and marshmallow creme until melted and well blended. Add vanilla and nuts, if desired. Pour into a buttered 13"x9" baking pan. Cool completely and cut into squares. Store in an airtight container. Makes 2½ to 3 pounds.

*Paula Bonchak*
*Bonham, TX*

Summertime Strawberry Pie

# prize-winning desserts

Give in to those sweet cravings and set any one of these special treats in front of family & friends. Rich and creamy Coconut Cream Pie (page 284) tastes so good topped with mounds of fluffy meringue. Take your favorite pies to another level and prepare Tried & True Pie Dough (page 289). Use one crust now and freeze the other two for later. A slice of moist Chocolate Pound Cake (page 262) and a cup of hot coffee makes for a perfect ending. From cakes and pies to cookies and other sweet treats...be sure to leave plenty of room for dessert!

# Nana's Famous Coconut-Pineapple Cake

*The "secret" ingredient in this fabulous family favorite: lemon-lime soda.*

15¼-oz. can crushed pineapple in juice, undrained and divided

1½ c. butter, softened

3 c. sugar

5 eggs

½ c. lemon-lime soda

3 c. cake flour, sifted

1 t. lemon extract

1 t. vanilla extract

6-oz. pkg. frozen sweetened flaked coconut, thawed

Drain pineapple, reserving ¾ cup juice. Remove ¼ cup reserved juice for Cream Cheese Frosting, and reserve crushed pineapple for Pineapple Filling.

Beat butter in a large bowl at medium speed with an electric mixer until creamy; gradually add sugar, beating well. Add eggs, one at a time, beating until blended after each addition. Combine ½ cup reserved pineapple juice and lemon-lime soda. Add flour to butter mixture alternately with juice mixture, beginning and ending with flour. Beat at low speed until blended after each addition. Stir in extracts. Pour batter into 3 greased and floured 9" round cake pans lined with wax paper. Bake at 350 degrees for 25 to 30 minutes, until a toothpick inserted near center comes out clean. Remove from pans immediately; cool on wire racks one hour.

Spread ¾ cup Pineapple Filling between cake layers; spread remaining filling on top of cake. Spread Cream Cheese Frosting on sides of cake. Sprinkle top and sides of cake with coconut. Serves 10 to 12.

## Pineapple Filling:

2 c. sugar

¼ c. cornstarch

1 c. water

1 c. reserved crushed pineapple, drained

Stir together sugar and cornstarch in a medium saucepan. Stir in water and pineapple; cook over low heat, stirring occasionally, for 15 minutes, or until mixture is thickened. Let cool completely.

## Cream Cheese Frosting:

½ c. butter, softened
3-oz. pkg. cream cheese,
    softened

16-oz. pkg. powdered sugar, sifted
¼ c. reserved pineapple juice
1 tsp. vanilla extract

Beat butter and cream cheese at medium speed with an electric mixer until creamy. Gradually add powdered sugar, juice and vanilla; mix well.

# Strawberry Layer Cake

6-oz. pkg. strawberry gelatin
    mix
½ c. hot water
18¼-oz. pkg. white cake mix

2 T. all-purpose flour
1 c. strawberries, hulled and
    chopped
4 eggs

Dissolve dry gelatin mix in hot water in a large bowl; cool. Add dry cake mix, flour and strawberries; mix well. Add eggs, one at a time, beating slightly after each addition. Pour batter into 3 greased and floured 8" round cake pans. Bake at 350 degrees for 20 minutes, or until toothpick inserted near center comes out clean. Let cool one hour. Spread Strawberry Frosting between layers and on top and sides of cake. Serves 12.

## Strawberry Frosting:

¼ c. butter, softened
3¾ to 5 c. powdered sugar

⅓ c. strawberries, hulled and
    finely chopped

Blend together butter and powdered sugar, adding sugar to desired consistency. Add strawberries; blend thoroughly.

*Steven Wilson*
*Chesterfield, VA*

Spring was always a wonderful time of year growing up in North Carolina. I remember going with Grandma to the strawberry farm to pick those huge, luscious red berries, often eating as many as we put in the basket!
—Steven

# Chocolate Pound Cake

12-oz. pkg. milk chocolate chips
½ c. butter, softened
2 c. sugar
4 eggs
2 t. vanilla extract
1 c. buttermilk

2 T. water
2½ c. all-purpose flour
½ t. salt
¼ t. baking soda
Optional: whipped cream, cocoa

Melt chocolate in a saucepan over low heat; remove from heat and set aside. Beat together butter and sugar in a large mixing bowl at medium speed with an electric mixer until light and fluffy. Add eggs, one at a time, beating well after each addition. Blend in melted chocolate and vanilla. Mix together buttermilk and water; set aside. Combine flour, salt and baking soda; add to chocolate mixture alternately with buttermilk mixture. Pour batter into a greased and floured Bundt® pan. Bake at 325 degrees for one hour and 20 minutes, until a toothpick inserted near center comes out clean. Cool for 10 minutes; remove from pan to wire rack. Let cool one hour. Garnish with whipped cream and sprinkle with cocoa, if desired. Serves 12 to 16.

*Sandy Groezinger*
*Stockton, IL*

## easy festive garnishes

Try these easy and memorable dessert topping ideas... gummy candies, conversation hearts, mini chocolate chips, candy sprinkles or a drizzle of chocolate syrup. Sweet and simple!

# Blueberry-Citrus Cake

18¼-oz. pkg. lemon cake mix
½ c. plus 2 T. orange juice,
    divided
1 c. water
⅓ c. oil
3 eggs, beaten

1½ c. fresh or frozen blueberries
1 T. orange zest
1 T. lemon zest
1 c. powdered sugar
Garnish: lemon and orange zest

Combine cake mix, ½ cup orange juice, water, oil and eggs in a large bowl. Beat with an electric mixer at low speed for 30 seconds. Increase speed to medium; beat for 2 minutes. With a wooden spoon, gently fold in blueberries and zests. Pour batter into a greased and floured Bundt® pan. Bake at 350 degrees for 35 to 40 minutes, until a toothpick inserted near center comes out clean. Cool completely in pan on a wire rack. Remove from pan. Blend remaining orange juice and powdered sugar until smooth; drizzle over cake. Sprinkle with zests. Serves 10 to 12.

# Sunshine Angel Food Cake

6 eggs, separated
⅜ t. salt, divided
½ t. cream of tartar
1 t. vanilla extract
1½ c. sugar, divided

1¼ c. all-purpose flour, divided
¼ c. cold water
1 t. baking powder
½ t. lemon extract

In a bowl, beat egg whites with an electric mixer at medium speed until foamy. Add ¼ teaspoon salt, cream of tartar and vanilla; beat at high speed until stiff peaks form. Mix in ¾ cup sugar and ½ cup flour; pour batter into an ungreased 10" tube pan. Beat egg yolks in a separate large bowl until lemon colored. Add water, baking powder, lemon extract and remaining salt, sugar and flour; mix well. Carefully, fold in yolk mixture. Bake at 350 degrees for 50 to 60 minutes. Run a knife around cake to loosen edges. Invert pan on wire rack and let cool one hour, until completely cool. Serves 10.

Blueberry-Citrus Cake

# Grandma's Banana Cupcakes

*You can drizzle jarred caramel sauce over the tops to make these yummy cupcakes extra special.*

½ c. butter, softened
1¾ c. sugar
2 eggs
2 c. all-purpose flour
1 t. baking powder
1 t. baking soda

¼ t. salt
1 c. buttermilk
2 bananas, mashed
1 t. vanilla extract
Optional: 24 toasted pecan
      halves, sliced banana

In a large bowl, beat butter and sugar with an electric mixer at medium speed, until light and fluffy. Add eggs, one at a time, beating after each addition. Combine flour, baking powder, baking soda and salt; add to batter alternately with buttermilk, beginning and ending with flour mixture. Beat at low speed after each addition until blended. Stir in bananas and vanilla. Fill paper-lined muffin cups ½ full. Bake at 350 degrees for 18 to 25 minutes, until a toothpick inserted in center comes out clean. Remove to wire racks to cool completely; frost with Cream Cheese Frosting. Store frosted cupcakes in an airtight container in refrigerator. Garnish each cupcake with a pecan half and banana slice just before serving, if desired. Makes 1½ to 2 dozen.

## Cream Cheese Frosting:

8-oz. pkg. cream cheese, softened
½ c. butter, softened
1 t. vanilla extract

⅛ t. salt
16-oz. pkg. powdered sugar

In a large bowl, beat cream cheese, butter, vanilla and salt with an electric mixer at medium speed, until creamy. Gradually add powdered sugar, beating until fluffy.

*Kelly Marcum*
*Rock Falls, IL*

# Chocolate-Zucchini Cupcakes

2 c. zucchini, shredded
3 eggs, beaten
2 c. sugar
¾ c. oil
2 t. vanilla extract
2 c. all-purpose flour

⅔ c. baking cocoa
1 t. salt
1 t. baking soda
½ t. baking powder
¾ c. milk chocolate chips

Stir together zucchini, eggs, sugar, oil and vanilla in a large bowl. Add remaining ingredients except chips; stir in chocolate chips. Spoon batter into 24 paper-lined muffin cups, filling muffin cups ⅔ full. Bake at 325 degrees for 25 minutes, or until a toothpick inserted near center comes out clean. Cool in pans on wire racks for 5 minutes. Remove from pans; cool completely. Frost with Peanut Butter Frosting. Makes 2 dozen.

## Peanut Butter Frosting:

½ c. creamy peanut butter
⅓ c. butter, softened
1 T. milk

½ t. vanilla extract
1½ c. powdered sugar

In a large bowl, beat all ingredients except sugar with an electric mixer at medium speed, until smooth. Gradually beat in powdered sugar. Stir in a little more milk, if necessary, to reach desired consistency.

*Michelle Rooney*
*Sunbury, OH*

# Mixed-Up Cupcakes

*Yes, you really do frost these cupcakes before baking!*

⅓ c. butter, softened
1 c. sugar
2 eggs, separated and divided
½ c. milk
1 t. vanilla extract
1⅔ c. all-purpose flour

2 t. baking powder
½ t. salt
½ c. light brown sugar, packed
2 T. baking cocoa
¼ c. chopped pecans

In a bowl, beat butter and sugar with an electric mixer at medium speed, until smooth. Beat one egg, one yolk, milk and vanilla into butter mixture; mix well. Sift together flour, baking powder and salt; stir into butter mixture until smooth. Fill paper-lined muffin cups ½ full; set aside. In a separate bowl, beat remaining egg white with an electric mixer at high speed, until stiff peaks form. Add brown sugar and cocoa to egg white; beat until well blended. Spoon a generous teaspoonful over each cupcake; sprinkle with nuts. Bake at 350 degrees for 20 minutes. Makes 12 to 15.

*Janie Saey*
*Wentzville, MO*

## cheap & easy

Cute napkin cuff in minutes. Use pinking shears to cut out a rectangle of fabric and wrap it around a napkin. Keep the ends in place with a perky flower brad, easily found in crafts stores. Simply cut an "X" in the rectangle of fabric and put the brad through the hole.

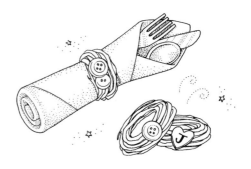

# Caramel-Glazed Apple Cake

*This made-from-scratch cake with its luscious glaze is irresistible! It's also easy to tote to holiday get-togethers or potlucks in its baking pan.*

1½ c. butter, softened
1 c. sugar
1 c. brown sugar, packed
3 eggs
3 c. all-purpose flour
2 t. cinnamon
1 t. baking soda

½ t. nutmeg
½ t. salt
5 Granny Smith apples, cored, peeled and diced
1¼ c. chopped pecans
2¼ t. vanilla extract

In a large bowl, beat butter and sugars with an electric mixer at medium-high speed, until light and fluffy. Add eggs, one at a time, beating after each addition. In a separate bowl, combine flour, cinnamon, baking soda, nutmeg and salt. Gradually add flour mixture to butter mixture with a wooden spoon to form a very thick batter. Stir in remaining ingredients. Pour batter into a greased and floured 13"x9" baking pan. Bake at 325 degrees for 50 to 60 minutes, until a toothpick inserted in center comes out clean. Cool cake in pan on a wire rack for at least 10 minutes. Poke holes all over surface of cake with a fork. Pour warm Caramel Glaze over cake. Serve warm or cooled. Serves 16.

## Caramel Glaze:

¼ c. butter
¼ c. sugar
¼ c. brown sugar, packed

⅛ t. salt
½ c. whipping cream

Melt butter in a saucepan over medium-low heat. Add sugars and salt. Cook, stirring frequently, for 2 minutes. Stir in cream and bring to a boil. Cook, stirring constantly, for 2 minutes.

*Brenda Smith*
*Delaware, OH*

# Homemade Gingerbread Cake

*Your entire home will smell delicious when you bake this cake. Don't skip the sauce...it's what takes this recipe over the top!*

2 c. all-purpose flour
2 t. ground ginger
1 t. cinnamon
1 t. nutmeg
1 t. baking powder
1 t. baking soda
½ t. salt
¼ t. ground cloves
½ c. butter, softened
½ c. sugar
1 c. molasses
1 c. buttermilk
1 egg, beaten
Garnish: whipped topping

Combine first 8 ingredients in a large bowl. In a separate large bowl, beat butter and sugar with an electric mixer at medium speed until fluffy. Beat in molasses. Add flour mixture and buttermilk alternately to molasses mixture, beginning and ending with flour mixture. Beat at low speed after each addition until blended. Stir in egg. Spoon batter into a greased and floured 13"x9" baking pan. Bake at 350 degrees for 40 to 45 minutes, until a toothpick inserted in center comes out clean. To serve, cut cake into squares; top with Warm Vanilla Sauce and a dollop of whipped topping. Serves 12 to 15.

## Warm Vanilla Sauce:

1 c. brown sugar, packed
2 T. all-purpose flour
1 c. water
1 T. butter
½ t. vanilla extract
⅛ t. salt

Mix together sugar and flour in a saucepan. Add remaining ingredients; cook and stir over medium heat until thickened.

*Dee Ann Ice*
*Delaware, OH*

# Butterscotch Picnic Cake

½ c. butter, softened
1 c. brown sugar, packed
3 eggs, beaten
1 t. vanilla extract
2 c. all-purpose flour
1 t. baking soda

1 t. salt
1½ c. buttermilk
1 c. quick-cooking oats,
    uncooked
6-oz. pkg. butterscotch chips
⅓ c. chopped walnuts

In a bowl, beat butter and brown sugar with an electric mixer at medium speed, until light and fluffy. Add eggs, one at a time, beating after each addition. Add vanilla. Whisk together flour, baking soda and salt; add to butter mixture alternately with buttermilk, blending well after each addition. Beat at low speed until blended. Stir in oats. Pour into a greased 13"x9" baking pan. Combine butterscotch chips and nuts; sprinkle over top. Bake at 350 degrees for 30 to 35 minutes. Cool completely in pan on a wire rack. Serves 15 to 18.

*Cindy Neel*
*Gooseberry Patch*

I share this recipe in memory of my grandmother, Blanche Crago. It was in her collection that she gathered from family & friends.

—Cindy

# Pecan Cheesecake Pie

½ 14.1-oz. pkg. refrigerated
   pie crusts
8-oz. pkg. cream cheese, softened
4 eggs, divided
¾ c. sugar, divided

2 t. vanilla extract, divided
¼ t. salt
1¼ c. chopped pecans
1 c. light corn syrup

Fit pie crust into a 9" pie plate according to package directions. Fold edges under and crimp. Beat cream cheese, one egg, ½ cup sugar, one teaspoon vanilla and salt with an electric mixer at medium speed until smooth. Pour cream cheese mixture into pie crust; sprinkle evenly with chopped pecans. Whisk together corn syrup and remaining 3 eggs, ¼ cup sugar and one teaspoon vanilla; pour mixture over pecans. Place pie on a baking sheet.

Bake at 350 degrees on lowest oven rack 50 to 55 minutes, until pie is set. Cool on a wire rack one hour or until completely cool. Serve immediately or cover and chill up to 2 days. Serves 8.

## keep the scraps

Let the kids make a sweet treat while waiting for a pie to bake! Twist scraps of leftover pie crust and roll in cinnamon-sugar. Bake at 350 degrees for 10 minutes, or until toasty.

# Baked Custard

1 c. evaporated milk
1 c. water
4 egg yolks

⅓ c. sugar
¼ t. salt
½ t. vanilla extract

Combine milk and water in a saucepan; heat just to boiling and set aside. Beat egg yolks slightly in a bowl; add sugar and salt. Gradually add hot milk mixture to eggs, stirring constantly. Stir in vanilla. Divide among 4 custard cups; set in a pan of hot water. Bake at 325 degrees for 50 minutes, or until a knife tip inserted in center comes out clean. Serve warm or chilled. Serves 4.

*Stephanie Mayer*
*Portsmouth, VA*

## warm surprise

Slip a packet of spiced cider, cocoa or herbal tea into a card for a special friend...she'll be absolutely delighted.

# Oma's Lemon Cheesecake

1½ c. all-purpose flour
2¼ c. sugar, divided
½ c. butter, softened
4 eggs, divided
1 T. milk
2 t. vanilla extract, divided
1 t. baking powder

½ t. salt
2 8-oz. pkgs. cream cheese, softened
16-oz. container sour cream, divided
zest of 1 lemon, divided

Combine flour, ⅔ cup sugar, butter, 2 eggs, milk, one teaspoon vanilla, baking powder and salt in a large bowl; mix well. Press evenly into the bottom and partially up the sides of a lightly greased 9" round springform pan. Blend cream cheese with 1⅓ cups of remaining sugar until smooth. Beat in remaining eggs, one at a time, beating slightly after each addition; stir in one cup sour cream, remaining vanilla and ⅔ of lemon zest. Pour cream cheese filling into crust; bake at 325 degrees for one hour. Turn off oven; leave pan in oven for 15 minutes. Mix together remaining sour cream, ¼ cup sugar and zest until smooth. Spread sour cream topping over filling. Set oven temperature to 325 degrees. Bake at 325 degrees for 15 more minutes. Cool on wire rack for one hour. Cover and chill 8 hours. Serves 12.

*Cora Wilfinger*
*Manitowoc, WI*

This is a treasured recipe, handed down from my oma (German for grandma) all the way to my daughter. This wonderful treat has been present at every Christmas in my life...not a crumb is left on the plate! The cake crust makes this so elegant and the cheesy, light, lemony goodness shines through. It is so worth the extra steps!

—Cora

# Cherry-Pecan Bread Pudding

2-lb. loaf French bread,
   cubed
4 c. milk
2 c. half-and-half
¾ c. plus 2 T. sugar, divided
6 eggs, beaten

2 t. vanilla extract
½ t. cinnamon
½ c. dried tart cherries
½ c. chopped pecans
½ c. butter, melted

Spread bread cubes on a baking sheet; let dry overnight. Combine milk, half-and-half and 7 tablespoons sugar in a saucepan over low heat. Heat to 120 degrees on a candy thermometer; remove from heat. Whisk together eggs, vanilla, cinnamon and remaining sugar in a large bowl. Stir in cherries and pecans. Slowly whisk half of milk mixture into egg mixture; add remaining milk mixture. Stir in bread cubes; toss to mix and let stand for 5 minutes. Mix in butter; transfer mixture to a lightly greased 13"x9" baking pan. Bake at 350 degrees for 35 minutes, or until center is firm. Serve warm. Serves 8 to 10.

# Chocolate Bread Pudding

2 c. milk
6 slices white bread, crusts
   trimmed
½ c. sugar
⅓ c. baking cocoa
2 eggs, separated and divided

2 T. butter, melted
1 t. vanilla extract
½ c. semi-sweet chocolate
   chunks
Garnish: whipped cream, baking
   cocoa

Heat milk in a large saucepan just until tiny bubbles form; remove from heat. Cube bread and add to milk; stir until combined. Add sugar, cocoa and egg yolks; stir until well blended. Add butter and vanilla. Beat egg whites until stiff peaks form; fold egg whites and chocolate chunks into chocolate mixture. Pour into 6 lightly greased custard cups; set cups in a large baking pan filled with one inch of hot water. Bake at 350 degrees for 50 minutes, or until firm. Garnish each serving with a dollop of whipped cream and a dusting of cocoa. Serves 6.

Cherry-Pecan Bread Pudding

# Dianna's Best Tiramisu

*I have tried many versions of this dessert…this one is by far the best. Everyone always asks for seconds…and the recipe!*

1 c. brewed coffee, cooled
½ c. plus 1 T. sugar, divided
2 8-oz. pkgs. cream cheese, softened
2 T. almond-flavored liqueur or ¼ to ½ t. almond extract
12-oz. container frozen whipped topping, thawed
16-oz. pound cake, cut into 30 slices
1 T. baking cocoa

Combine coffee and one tablespoon sugar in a medium bowl; set aside. In a bowl, beat cream cheese with an electric mixer at medium speed, until fluffy. Add remaining sugar and almond liqueur or extract. Gently fold in whipped topping and set aside. Layer 10 cake slices on the bottom of an ungreased 13"x9" baking pan. Brush one-third of coffee mixture over cake slices with a pastry brush. Top with one-third of cream cheese mixture. Repeat 2 more times to create 3 layers. Sprinkle cocoa over top and chill overnight. Serves 16 to 24.

*Dianna Oakland*
*Titusville, FL*

## along the rim

Dip the rim of a mug into melted chocolate and then quickly dip the rim in crushed peppermints. Fill the mug with creamy cocoa and marshmallows and then sit back and enjoy.

# People-Pleasin' Peach Pie

2 9-inch pie crusts
8 c. peaches, peeled, pitted and
    sliced
2 t. lemon juice
1 t. vanilla extract
1 c. sugar
6 T. cornstarch

1 t. cinnamon
¼ t. nutmeg
¼ t. salt
4 T. butter, sliced
1 to 2 T. milk
Optional: whipped cream

Line a 9" pie plate with one crust and set aside. Combine peaches, lemon juice and vanilla in a large bowl. Mix sugar, cornstarch, spices and salt in a separate bowl. Add sugar mixture to peach mixture; toss gently to coat. Spoon into pie crust; dot with butter. With a small cookie cutter, cut vents in remaining crust, reserving cut-outs. Place crust on top of pie; trim and seal edges. Brush milk over top crust and cut-outs; arrange cut-outs on crust. Cover edges loosely with aluminum foil. Bake at 400 degrees for 40 minutes. Remove foil and bake 10 to 15 more minutes, until crust is golden and filling is bubbly. Garnish with whipped cream, if desired. Serves 6 to 8.

*Kay Marone*
*Des Moines, IA*

A positively perfect peach pie my mom taught me how to make for when the sun is shining and the peaches are ripe.

—Kay

## not just for veggies

Toting a pie to a picnic or party? A bamboo steamer from an import store is just the thing...it can even hold two pies at once.

# Coconut Cream Pie

*I have such fond memories of when my dad's family would all get together to eat at a local restaurant. Their coconut cream pie was one of my favorites! This is my own version.*

2 c. milk
⅔ c. sugar
¼ c. cornstarch
¼ t. salt
3 egg yolks, beaten

1½ c. sweetened flaked coconut, divided
2 T. butter, softened
½ t. vanilla extract
9-inch pie crust, baked

Combine milk, sugar, cornstarch and salt in a large saucepan; cook over medium heat until thickened, stirring constantly. Remove from heat. Place egg yolks in a small bowl. Stir a small amount of hot milk mixture into egg yolks. Pour yolk mixture back into saucepan; simmer gently for 2 minutes. Finely chop one cup coconut; combine with butter and vanilla and then blend with yolk mixture. Pour into crust. Spread Meringue over hot pie filling; seal to edges. Sprinkle with remaining coconut. Bake at 350 degrees for 12 minutes. Serves 8.

## Meringue:

4 egg whites

7-oz. jar marshmallow creme

In a bowl, beat egg whites with an electric mixer at high speed, until very stiff peaks form. Add marshmallow creme; beat for 4 minutes.

*Lauren Williams*
*Kewanee, MO*

# Banana Cream Pie

½ c. sliced almonds, toasted
   and divided
9-inch graham cracker crust
3 to 4 bananas, sliced
3 T. cornstarch
¼ t. salt
1⅔ c. water
14-oz. can sweetened condensed
   milk

3 egg yolks, beaten
2 T. butter
1 t. vanilla extract
12-oz. container frozen whipped
   topping, thawed
Garnish: additional banana
   slices

Set aside some almonds for garnish. Line the bottom and sides of pie crust with banana slices. Sprinkle with remaining almonds; set aside. Dissolve cornstarch and salt in water in a saucepan over medium heat. Stir in condensed milk and egg yolks. Cook, stirring constantly, until thickened and bubbly, about 7 minutes. Remove from heat; stir in butter and vanilla. Cool slightly; spoon into crust. Cover and refrigerate for at least 4 hours. At serving time, cover with whipped topping; garnish with reserved sliced almonds and extra banana slices. Serves 8.

*Caroline Pacheco*
*Stafford, VA*

My mother and I have been making this dreamy pie since I was a young girl...it's one of my father's favorites. Now I'm a mother of two little girls myself, and I make it with them every Thanksgiving holiday. I hope you enjoy it as much as we do!

—Caroline

# Green Tomato Pie

*You'll be surprised how much the tomatoes in this pie taste like apples.*

If you still have lots of green tomatoes and the first frost is on its way, bring them inside to ripen. Arrange the tomatoes inside a cardboard box lined with shredded paper. Top the tomatoes with a layer of newspaper...in about 3 to 4 weeks, they'll be rosy red.

4 c. green tomatoes, peeled and
    sliced
1 T. lemon juice
1½ c. sugar
3 T. all-purpose flour
1 t. cinnamon
⅛ t. salt
2 9-inch pie crusts

Place tomatoes in a colander to drain; toss with lemon juice. Whisk together sugar, flour, cinnamon and salt; sprinkle over tomatoes and toss to coat. Place one crust in a 9" pie plate; spoon in filling. Top with remaining crust; flute edges and vent as desired. Bake at 450 degrees for 15 minutes; reduce oven temperature to 350 degrees and bake 45 to 60 more minutes. Serves 6 to 8.

*Abigail Bunce*
*Drain, OR*

# Summertime Strawberry Pie

(pictured on page 258)

1 qt. strawberries, hulled and
    divided
1 c. sugar
3 T. cornstarch
3-oz. pkg. cream cheese,
    softened
9-inch pie crust, baked
Optional: whipped cream

Reserve half of the biggest strawberries; set aside. Place remaining strawberries, about 1½ cups, in a blender. Process until smooth. Add water to puréed berries, if needed, to equal 2 cups; pour into a small saucepan. Add sugar and cornstarch; bring to a boil, stirring, and cook for one minute. Remove from heat; cool. Spread cream cheese in bottom of pie crust; arrange reserved berries on top, pointed-end up. Pour cooled strawberry sauce over top. Cover and chill for 2 hours. Top with whipped cream, if desired. Serves 8 to 10.

*Christina Hubbell*
*Jackson, MI*

Green Tomato Pie

Sweet Apple Tarts

# Sweet Apple Tarts

1 sheet frozen puff pastry,
    thawed
½ c. apricot jam
3 to 4 Granny Smith apples,
    cored, peeled and very thinly
    sliced

⅓ c. brown sugar, packed
½ t. cinnamon
½ c. pistachio nuts, chopped
Optional: vanilla ice cream

A delicious can't-fail recipe that's perfect for any occasion! Cut the pastry squares with a fluted pastry wheel for a pretty finish.

Roll pastry into a 12-inch square on a lightly floured surface. Cut pastry into nine, 3-inch squares. Arrange squares on an ungreased baking sheet; pierce with a fork. Spoon jam evenly over each square; arrange apple slices over jam. Combine brown sugar and cinnamon in a small bowl; mix well. Sprinkle over apple slices. Bake at 400 degrees for 20 to 25 minutes, until pastry is golden and apples are crisp-tender. Sprinkle with nuts. Serve warm topped with scoops of ice cream, if desired. Serves 9.

*Jill Ball*
*Highland, UT*


# Tried & True Pie Dough

*My mother always makes about 13 to 15 pies during the holidays. This is the best dough and so very easy to work with.*

3½ c. all-purpose flour
2 c. shortening
1 T. sugar

1 egg, beaten
½ c. cold water
1 T. vinegar

Blend together flour, shortening and sugar in a large bowl. Beat together remaining ingredients in a separate bowl. Add egg mixture to flour mixture; blend together. Divide into 3 balls; roll each out on a lightly floured surface. Makes 3 pie crusts.

*Sadie Phelan*
*Connellsville, PA*

# Easy Cherry Cobbler

*If they're available, use fresh-from-the-farm cherries for a special treat. Don't forget to pit them!*

15-oz. can tart red cherries,
   undrained
1 c. all-purpose flour
1¼ c. sugar, divided
1 c. milk

2 t. baking powder
⅛ t. salt
½ c. butter, melted
Optional: vanilla ice cream or
   whipped cream

Bring cherries to a boil in a saucepan over medium heat; remove from heat. Mix flour, one cup sugar, milk, baking powder and salt in a medium bowl. Pour butter into 6 one-cup ramekins or into a 2-quart casserole dish; pour flour mixture over butter. Add cherries; do not stir. Sprinkle remaining sugar over top. Bake at 400 degrees for 20 to 30 minutes. Serve warm with ice cream or whipped cream, if desired. Serves 4 to 6.

*Melonie Klosterhoff*
*Fairbanks, AK*

## get them while they last

Be sure to pick up a pint of ice cream in pumpkin, cinnamon and other delicious seasonal flavors when they're available...they add that special touch to holiday meals!

Brenda's Fruit Crisp

# Brenda's Fruit Crisp

5 c. frozen peaches, apples or
    berries, thawed and juices
    reserved
2 to 4 T. sugar
½ c. long-cooking oats, uncooked
½ c. brown sugar, packed
¼ c. all-purpose flour
¼ t. nutmeg
¼ t. cinnamon
¼ t. vanilla extract
Optional: ¼ c. sweetened flaked
    coconut
¼ c. butter, diced
Optional: vanilla ice cream

Place fruit and juices in an ungreased 2-quart casserole dish; stir in sugar and set aside. Mix oats, sugar, flour, nutmeg, cinnamon and vanilla in a medium bowl. Stir in coconut, if desired. Add butter to oat mixture; combine until mixture is the texture of coarse crumbs. Sprinkle over fruit. Bake at 375 degrees for 30 to 35 minutes, until topping is golden and fruit is tender. Serve warm topped with ice cream, if desired. Serves 6.

# Blackberry Crumble

⅔ c. butter, softened
1½ c. quick-cooking oats,
    uncooked
1⅓ c. all-purpose flour
1 c. brown sugar, packed
½ t. baking soda
1 qt. blackberries
¾ c. sugar
3 T. cornstarch
⅛ t. salt
Optional: vanilla ice cream or
    whipped cream

Mix together butter, oats, flour, brown sugar and baking soda in a medium bowl with a fork until pea-sized crumbles form; set aside. Combine blackberries, sugar, cornstarch and salt in a large heavy saucepan. Gently mash some berries, leaving about half of them whole. Bring to a boil over medium-high heat, stirring constantly. Reduce heat to medium; cook until mixture thickens.

Pour into a lightly greased 13'x9" glass baking pan; crumble topping over berries. Bake at 350 degrees for 30 minutes, or until lightly golden. Serve with ice cream or whipped cream, if desired. Serves 8 to 10.

# Mulberry Buckle

*Come July, we pick mulberries from the tree in our backyard... perfect for Pioneer Day or a family night treat. It's equally good with fresh raspberries or blackberries.*

*—Mary*

2 c. all-purpose flour
2½ t. baking powder
¼ t. salt
½ c. butter, softened

¾ c. sugar
1 egg, beaten
½ c. milk
2 c. mulberries

Stir together flour, baking powder and salt in a medium bowl; set aside. In a bowl, beat butter and sugar with an electric mixer at medium speed, until light and fluffy. Add egg and beat well. Add flour mixture and milk alternately to egg mixture, beginning and ending with flour mixture. Beat at low speed after each addition until blended. Pour into a greased 9"x9" baking pan; top with mulberries and Crumb Topping. Bake at 350 degrees for 50 to 60 minutes, until golden. Serve warm. Serves 9.

## Crumb Topping:

½ c. all-purpose flour
½ c. sugar

½ t. cinnamon
¼ c. butter

Sift together flour, sugar and cinnamon. Cut in butter until mixture resembles coarse crumbs.

*Mary Murray*
*Gooseberry Patch*

## leafy trivets

Protect your table from hot dishes with leaf trivets. They're easily made from wool felt. Simply cut out oversize leaves in any shape you like (you can use a disappearing-ink fabric pen to make a pattern before cutting). When ready to use, simply layer them down the center of the table where hot dishes will be placed.

# Southern Oatmeal Cookies

*These are the best oatmeal cookies you'll ever taste. They're great with a glass of cold milk.*

1 c. butter, softened
1 c. sugar
1 c. brown sugar, packed
2 eggs
1 t. vanilla extract

1½ c. all-purpose flour
1 t. baking soda
1 t. salt
3 c. long-cooking oats, uncooked
1 c. chopped walnuts or pecans

In a large bowl, beat butter and sugars with an electric mixer at medium speed, until fluffy. Beat in eggs, one at a time, blending well after each addition. Add vanilla; set aside. Sift together flour, baking soda and salt. Fold flour mixture into butter mixture; stir in oats and nuts. Form rounded teaspoonfuls into balls and place on greased baking sheets 2 inches apart. Bake at 350 degrees for 5 to 7 minutes. Let stand on baking sheets for 4 to 5 minutes before removing to wire racks to cool completely. Store in an airtight container. Makes 4 dozen.

*Dawn Fannin*
*Ravenna, TX*

## nuttier taste

For a toasty, nutty flavor, bake oats before using them in cookies. Simply spread them on an ungreased baking sheet and bake at 300 degrees for 10 to 12 minutes... cool slightly before stirring into cookie dough.

# Lemon-Macadamia Cookies

*One of my daughters, Lisa, loves macadamia nuts, and I love lemon; so I combined our favorite flavors to create these scrumptious cookies.*

¾ c. butter, softened
1 c. sugar
1 c. brown sugar, packed
2 eggs
3.4-oz. pkg. instant lemon
   pudding mix
2¼ c. all-purpose flour

1 t. baking soda
¼ t. salt
2 t. lemon zest
1 t. lemon extract
1 c. macadamia nuts, coarsely
   chopped
½ c. toffee baking bits

In a large bowl, beat butter and sugars with an electric mixer at medium speed, until light and fluffy. Add eggs, one at a time, beating until blended after each addition. Combine dry pudding mix, flour, baking soda, salt and zest in a separate bowl. Slowly add pudding mixture to butter mixture. Add extract; beat until combined. Stir in nuts and toffee bits. Drop by rounded tablespoonfuls onto ungreased baking sheets 2 inches apart. Bake at 350 degrees for 10 to 12 minutes, until lightly golden around edges. Cool cookies on baking sheets for 2 minutes. Remove to wire racks to cool completely. Store in an airtight container. Makes 4 dozen.

*Brenda Melancon*
*Gonzales, LA*

## so versatile

A one-gallon glass apothecary jar makes a great cookie jar. Before using, thoroughly wash jar with hot soap and water and dry completely. Personalize it by using a glass paint pen to add a message such as "Family Favorite Cookies." Add hearts or swirls just for fun.

# Spicy Maple-Anise Snaps

1 c. butter, softened
1 c. sugar
1 c. dark brown sugar, packed
1 egg, beaten
1 t. maple extract
2½ c. all-purpose flour

1 T. ground anise seed
1 t. baking soda
1 t. cinnamon
¾ t. ground cloves
½ c. pecans, finely chopped

In a large bowl, beat butter and sugars with an electric mixer at medium speed, until fluffy. Beat in egg and extract; set aside. Combine flour and remaining ingredients except nuts in a separate bowl; mix well. Gradually blend flour mixture into butter mixture; beat at low speed until blended. Add pecans and mix in well.

Divide dough into 3 parts; form each into a log 8 inches long. Wrap tightly in wax paper; chill one hour, or until very firm. Remove one roll at a time from refrigerator and slice ¼-inch thick. Place one to 2 inches apart on parchment paper-lined baking sheets.

Bake at 375 degrees for 10 to 12 minutes, until golden. Immediately remove cookies from baking sheets; cool completely on wire racks. Store in airtight containers. Flavors will become more pronounced over the next several days. Makes 7 dozen.

*Judy Gillham*
*Whittier, CA*

# Sour Cream Drop Cookies

¾ c. butter, softened
1½ c. sugar
2 eggs, beaten
1 t. vanilla extract
½ t. lemon or orange extract

8-oz. container sour cream
3 c. all-purpose flour
1 t. baking powder
1 t. baking soda

*The citrus extract makes these taste extra special.*

In a large bowl, beat butter and sugar with an electric mixer at medium speed, until fluffy. Add eggs, vanilla and lemon or orange extract; mix well. Fold in sour cream; set aside. Combine remaining ingredients in a separate bowl; gradually add to butter mixture. Drop by teaspoonfuls onto greased baking sheets. Bake at 350 degrees for 10 to 12 minutes. Remove to wire racks and cool completely. Store in an airtight container. Makes 3 dozen.

*Cheryl Bastian*
*Northumberland, PA*


# Chocolate Fudge Cookies

2 6-oz. pkgs. semi-sweet
   chocolate chips
¼ c. butter
14-oz. can sweetened condensed
   milk

1 t. vanilla extract
1 c. all-purpose flour
1 c. chopped nuts

Combine chocolate chips, butter and condensed milk in a microwave-safe bowl; microwave on high 2 to 3 minutes or until melted, stirring every 30 seconds. Add vanilla, flour and nuts. Drop by teaspoonfuls onto greased baking sheets. Bake at 350 degrees for 7 minutes. Remove to wire racks and cool completely. Makes 5 to 6 dozen.

*Karen Adams*
*Cincinnati, OH*

# Gooey Toffee Scotchies

18¼-oz. pkg. yellow cake mix
½ c. brown sugar, packed
½ c. butter, melted and slightly
   cooled
2 eggs, beaten
1 c. cashews, chopped
8-oz. pkg. toffee baking bits

In a bowl, beat dry cake mix, brown sugar, butter and eggs with an electric mixer at medium speed for one minute. Stir in cashews. Press mixture into the bottom of a greased 15"x10" jelly-roll pan; sprinkle with toffee bits. Bake at 350 degrees for 15 to 20 minutes, until a toothpick inserted in center comes out clean. Cool in pan and cut into bars or triangles. To serve, drizzle with warm Toffee Sauce. Makes about 2½ dozen.

## Toffee Sauce:

¾ c. plus 1 T. dark brown sugar,
   packed
2 T. dark corn syrup
6 T. butter
⅔ c. whipping cream

Bring sugar, syrup and butter to a boil in a saucepan over medium heat. Cook for 2 minutes. Carefully stir in cream and simmer for 2 more minutes or until sauce thickens. Keep warm.

*Rhonda Reeder*
*Ellicott City, MD*

*I'm always looking for desserts with toffee in them. These delectable bars are my new favorites!*
—Rhonda

## stock up & save

By mid-autumn, you'll find grocery specials on many items needed for holiday baking...butter, chocolate chips, vanilla extract, candied fruits, brown sugar and flour.

# Chocolatey Chewy Brownies

To make your brownies picture worthy, try the following...trim the edges first and then wipe a very sharp knife with a damp cloth after each cut.

1 c. butter, softened
2 c. sugar
4 eggs, beaten
1 c. all-purpose flour
4 1-oz. sqs. unsweetened baking chocolate, melted
1 t. vanilla extract
1 c. chopped walnuts

In a bowl, beat butter and sugar with an electric mixer at medium speed, until creamy. Beat in eggs, mixing well. Stir in remaining ingredients. Pour into a greased and floured 13"x9" baking pan. Bake at 350 degrees for 30 minutes. Cool; cut into squares. Makes 1½ to 2 dozen.

*Jacklyn Akey*
*Merrill, WI*

# Nanny's Shortbread Chews

½ c. butter, softened
1½ c. brown sugar, packed and
    divided
1 c. plus 2 T. all-purpose flour,
    divided
2 eggs, beaten

1 t. baking powder
1 t. vanilla extract
½ t. salt
1½ c. chopped dates or raisins
1 c. chopped walnuts or pecans

Mix together butter, ½ cup brown sugar and one cup flour in a medium bowl until the consistency of fine crumbs. Press butter mixture into the bottom of a greased 13"x9" baking pan. Bake at 350 degrees for 8 to 10 minutes; remove from oven. Mix remaining brown sugar and flour, eggs, baking powder, vanilla and salt; blend well. Stir in dates or raisins and nuts; pour mixture over baked crust. Return to oven; bake 15 to 20 more minutes. Cool completely and cut into squares. Makes 2 dozen.

*Paula McFadden*
*Owensboro, KY*

My Aunt Nanny always had a batch of these cookies waiting for me whenever I came for a visit. I have her handwritten recipe framed in my kitchen to keep her close to my heart.

—Paula

# GG's Ladyfingers Candy

My husband's grandmother, GG, as she likes to be called, has always made this delicious candy for Christmas. Whenever visitors stop by, she pulls out a tin of candy for them to enjoy.

—Carol

16-oz. pkg. powdered sugar
2 c. sweetened flaked coconut
1 c. pecans or walnuts, finely chopped
1 c. graham cracker crumbs
1 c. marshmallow creme
1 c. creamy peanut butter
1 t. vanilla extract
1 c. butter, melted
12-oz. pkg. semi-sweet chocolate chips
½ bar paraffin wax, chopped

Combine first 7 ingredients in a large bowl. Pour butter over mixture; stir to combine. Chill one to 2 hours. Form tablespoonfuls of mixture into ladyfingers and place on wax paper-lined baking sheets. Chill one to 2 more hours. Combine chocolate chips and paraffin in the top of a double boiler over low heat. Stir until completely melted and smooth. Dip ladyfingers into chocolate with a fork. Allow excess chocolate to drip back into pan; place on wax paper to cool. Store in an airtight container in refrigerator. Makes about 5 dozen.

*Carol Hickman*
*Kingsport, TN*

# Beth's Caramel Corn

16 c. popped popcorn
1 c. butter
1⅔ c. brown sugar, packed
½ c. corn syrup

1 t. salt
½ t. baking soda
1 t. vanilla extract

Spray a roasting pan with non-stick vegetable spray. Place popcorn in pan; set aside. Melt butter in a large heavy saucepan over medium heat; stir in brown sugar, corn syrup and salt. Bring to a boil, stirring constantly. Stop stirring; continue to boil for exactly 5 minutes. Remove from heat; stir in baking soda and vanilla. Gradually pour hot mixture over popcorn; mix well. Cover and bake at 250 degrees for one hour, stirring every 15 minutes. Spread on parchment paper and cool completely. Break apart; store in an airtight container. Makes about 12 servings.

*Beth Hershey*
*Denver, PA*

One year I made this sweet, crunchy popcorn treat as gifts for my family...they all loved it!

—Beth

# Salted Nut Squares

16-oz. jar dry-roasted peanuts, divided
¼ c. butter
10-oz. pkg. peanut butter chips

14-oz. can sweetened condensed milk
10½-oz. pkg. marshmallows

Spread half of peanuts in a lightly greased 13"x9" baking pan. Combine butter, peanut butter chips and condensed milk in a saucepan over medium heat; stir until melted and well blended. Stir in marshmallows until melted; spread marshmallow mixture over peanuts. Sprinkle remaining peanuts over top; gently press down into marshmallow mixture. Cool; chill until set, about one hour. Slice into squares. Makes 2 dozen.

*Marcy Richardson*
*Robbinsdale, MN*

This is a family favorite on Halloween.

—Marcy

# Homemade Vanilla Ice Cream

*When I was young, we'd have what we called an "ice cream supper." We would pile in the car and head to the ice cream parlor…that really hit the spot on a hot summer night.*

2½ c. whipping cream
2 c. half-and-half
2 eggs, beaten
1 c. sugar

¼ t. salt
2¼ t. vanilla extract
Optional: whole strawberry

Combine all ingredients except vanilla in a heavy saucepan over medium-low heat, stirring constantly until mixture is thick enough to coat the back of a spoon and reaches 160 degrees on a candy thermometer. Remove from heat and stir in vanilla. Set pan in an ice-filled bowl; stir. Cover and chill 8 hours or up to 24 hours. Pour mixture into ice cream maker and freeze according to manufacturer's directions. Garnish with whole strawberry, if desired. Serves 12.

*Jill Valentine*
*Jackson, TN*

## pretty & edible

Accent a dessert with edible flowers…rose petals, nasturtiums, violets and pansies are some colorful choices. Make sure your flowers are pesticide-free and rinse them well before using.

# 16 splendid menus

## old-school lunch

*serves 4*

*Extra-Cheesy Grilled Cheese (page 108)*

*Easy Tomato Soup (page 98)*

*milk*

## ladies' garden party

*serves 8*

*\*Herb Garden Sandwiches (page 111)*

*Brown Sugar Fruit Dip (page 52)*

*Rosemary-Lemon-Pineapple Punch (page 77)*

*Oma's Lemon Cheesecake (page 277)*

*\* denotes double recipe*

# game-day celebration

*serves 8 to 10*

*The Best-Yet Buffalo Wings (page 59)*

*Dad's Chili-Cheese Ball (page 66)*

*Mexican Nacho Chips (page 56)*

*assorted beverages*

# Mother's Day breakfast

*serves 4 to 5*

*Nutty Maple Waffles (page 30)*

*Sweet & Spicy Bacon (page 26)*

*orange juice & coffee*

# Sunday supper

*serves 6*

*Mama's Meatloaf (page 148)*

*Herbed Mashed Potatoes (page 178)*

*Zesty Horseradish Carrots (page 184)*

*Easy Cherry Cobbler (page 290)*

# come on over!

*serves 8 to 10*

*Chinese Chicken Spread (page 51)*

*Julie's Fresh Guacamole (page 49)*

*\*4-Layer Mexican Dip (page 45)*

*Old-Fashioned Ginger Beer (page 79)*

*\* denotes double recipe*

# reunion picnic favorites

*serves 16*

*Lemony Orzo Salad (page 196)

*Ada's Famous Broccoli Salad (page 198)

Butterscotch Picnic Cake (page 273)

# southern veggie plate

*serves 4*

Mom's Macaroni & Cheese (page 177)

Fried Green Tomatoes (page 182)

Country-Style Pepper Cabbage (page 181)

cornbread

sweet tea

## Italian feast

*serves 6*

*Pasta e Fagioli (page 92)*

*Italian Zucchini Casserole (page 134)*

*mixed salad greens*

*Dianna's Best Tiramisu (page 281)*

## host a small gathering

*serves 8*

*Tuscan Pork Loin (page 161)*

*\*Pecan-Butternut Squash Bake (page 189)*

*Caramelized Brussels Sprouts (page 188)*

*\* denotes double recipe*

# elegant brunch

*serves 4 to 6*

*Crab, Corn & Pepper Frittata (page 12)*

*Bountiful Garden Salad (page 193)*

*Sunshine Angel Food Cake (page 264)*

# special dinner for Dad

*serves 4 to 6*

*Apple-Spice Country Ribs (page 221)*

*Confetti Coleslaw (page 190)*

*baked beans*

*Sweet Apple Tarts (page 289)*

# summer's curtain call

# soup swap

*\*denotes double recipe*

# best county fair desserts

*serves 6 to 8*

*Green Tomato Pie (page 286)*

*Coconut Cream Pie (page 284)*

*Brenda's Fruit Crisp (page 293)*

*People-Pleasin' Peach Pie (page 283)*

# a taste of Louisiana

*serves 6*

*Louisiana Red Beans & Rice (page 227)*

*Down-on-the-Bayou Gumbo (page 223)*

*Chocolate Bread Pudding (page 278)*

# METRIC EQUIVALENTS

The recipes that appear in this cookbook use the standard U.S. method for measuring liquid and dry or solid ingredients (teaspoons, tablespoons and cups). The information in the following charts is provided to help cooks outside the United States successfully use these recipes. All equivalents are approximate.

## METRIC EQUIVALENTS FOR DIFFERENT TYPES OF INGREDIENTS

A standard cup measure of a dry or solid ingredient will vary in weight depending on the type of ingredient.
A standard cup of liquid is the same volume for any type of liquid. Use the following chart when converting standard cup measures to grams (weight) or milliliters (volume).

| Standard Cup | Fine Powder (ex. flour) | Grain (ex. rice) | Granular (ex. sugar) | Liquid Solids (ex. butter) | Liquid (ex. milk) |
|---|---|---|---|---|---|
| 1 | 140 g | 150 g | 190 g | 200 g | 240 ml |
| ¾ | 105 g | 113 g | 143 g | 150 g | 180 ml |
| ⅔ | 93 g | 100 g | 125 g | 133 g | 160 ml |
| ½ | 70 g | 75 g | 95 g | 100 g | 120 ml |
| ⅓ | 47 g | 50 g | 63 g | 67 g | 80 ml |
| ¼ | 35 g | 38 g | 48 g | 50 g | 60 ml |
| ⅛ | 18 g | 19 g | 24 g | 25 g | 30 ml |

## USEFUL EQUIVALENTS FOR LIQUID INGREDIENTS BY VOLUME

| | | | | | | |
|---|---|---|---|---|---|---|
| ¼ tsp | = | | | | | 1 ml |
| ½ tsp | = | | | | | 2 ml |
| 1 tsp | = | | | | | 5 ml |
| 3 tsp | = | 1 tbls | | = | ½ fl oz | = | 15 ml |
| | | 2 tbls | = ⅛ cup | = | 1 fl oz | = | 30 ml |
| | | 4 tbls | = ¼ cup | = | 2 fl oz | = | 60 ml |
| | | 5⅓ tbls | = ⅓ cup | = | 3 fl oz | = | 80 ml |
| | | 8 tbls | = ½ cup | = | 4 fl oz | = | 120 ml |
| | | 10⅔ tbls | = ⅔ cup | = | 5 fl oz | = | 160 ml |
| | | 12 tbls | = ¾ cup | = | 6 fl oz | = | 180 ml |
| | | 16 tbls | = 1 cup | = | 8 fl oz | = | 240 ml |
| | | 1 pt | = 2 cups | = 16 fl oz | = | 480 ml |
| | | 1 qt | = 4 cups | = 32 fl oz | = | 960 ml |
| | | | | 33 fl oz | = | 1000 ml = 1 liter |

## USEFUL EQUIVALENTS FOR DRY INGREDIENTS BY WEIGHT

(To convert ounces to grams, multiply the number of ounces by 30.)

| | | | | |
|---|---|---|---|---|
| 1 oz | = | ¹⁄₁₆ lb | = | 30 g |
| 4 oz | = | ¼ lb | = | 120 g |
| 8 oz | = | ½ lb | = | 240 g |
| 12 oz | = | ¾ lb | = | 360 g |
| 16 oz | = | 1 lb | = | 480 g |

## USEFUL EQUIVALENTS FOR LENGTH

(To convert inches to centimeters, multiply the number of inches by 2.5.)

| | | | | |
|---|---|---|---|---|
| 1 in = | | = 2.5 cm | | |
| 6 in = | ½ ft | = 15 cm | | |
| 12 in = | 1 ft | = 30 cm | | |
| 36 in = | 3 ft = 1 yd | = 90 cm | | |
| 40 in = | | = 100 cm | = 1 meter | |

## USEFUL EQUIVALENTS FOR COOKING/OVEN TEMPERATURES

| | Fahrenheit | Celsius | Gas Mark |
|---|---|---|---|
| Freeze Water | 32° F | 0° C | |
| Room Temperature | 68° F | 20° C | |
| Boil Water | 212° F | 100° C | |
| Bake | 325° F | 160° C | 3 |
| | 350° F | 180° C | 4 |
| | 375° F | 190° C | 5 |
| | 400° F | 200° C | 6 |
| | 425° F | 220° C | 7 |
| | 450° F | 230° C | 8 |
| Broil | | | Grill |

# index

# Our Story

**B**ack in 1984 we were next-door neighbors raising our families in the little town of Delaware, Ohio. We were two moms with small children looking for a way to do what we loved and stay home with the kids too. We shared a love of home cooking and making memories with family & friends. After many a conversation over the backyard fence, **Gooseberry Patch** was born.

We put together the first catalog & cookbooks at our kitchen tables and packed boxes from the basement, enlisting the help of our loved ones wherever we could. From that little family, we've grown to include an amazing group of creative folks who love cooking, decorating and creating as much as we do.

Hard to believe it's been more than 25 years since those kitchen-table days. Today we're best known for our homestyle, family-friendly cookbooks. We love hand-picking the recipes and are tickled to share our inspiration, ideas and more with you. Our hope is that each book captures the stories and heart of all of you who have shared with us. Whether you've been along for the ride from the beginning or are just discovering us, welcome to our family!

*Your friends at Gooseberry Patch*

## We couldn't make our best-selling cookbooks without YOU!

Each of our books is filled with recipes from cooks just like you, gathered from kitchens all across the country.

Share your tried & true recipes with us on our website and you could be selected for an upcoming cookbook. If your recipe is included, you'll receive a FREE copy of the cookbook when it's published!

## www.gooseberrypatch.com

## We'd love to add YOU to our Circle of Friends!

Get free recipes, crafts, giveaways and so much more when you join our email club...join us online at all the spots below for even more goodies!

Join our Circle of Friends

Subscribe on YouTube

Find us on Facebook

Read Our Blog

Follow us on Twitter

Follow us on Pinterest